TRADITIONS OF CHRISTMAS

Traditions of CHRISTMAS

FROM THE EDITORS OF VICTORIA

83 press

Hoffman Media
2323 2nd Avenue North
Birmingham, AL 35203
hoffmanmedia.com

ISBN 9780983598497
Printed in China

CONTENTS

INTRODUCTION

As seen through the eyes of children, Christmas is nothing short of magical, with dreams of candy canes and reindeer paws and gifts mysteriously left beneath a bauble-laden tree. But for adults, time lends a deeper resonance to the day, when layers of sweet memories from Yuletides past are laced with the joy of family togetherness and a sacred reverence for the true meaning of the celebration. Whether the holiday comes wrapped up in traditional hues of red and green or glitters with sophisticated shades of silver and gold, one thing is certain: Christmas truly is the most wonderful time of the year.

With that sentiment in mind, the editors of *Victoria* magazine present our latest keepsake volume, *Traditions of Christmas*, brimming with page upon page of seasonal inspiration. Heralding the season with jubilance, we offer ideas for creating a festive welcome to your home and embrace the time-honored tradition of sending greeting cards. As the tree is often the center of holiday décor, you'll find a breathtaking cavalcade of the prettiest evergreens—each lovely branch laden with exquisite ornaments and twinkling lights. Impassioned homeowners open their doors wide, allowing glimpses into grand old residences where holiday customs of the past meet new ones in the making and treasured collections find pride of place amid the holly and the ivy.

Since entertaining goes hand in hand with the holidays, gracious tables and delectable menus take center stage this time of year. We present a selection of elegantly merry settings, accompanied by recipes certain to become new favorites. You'll also find ideas that embrace the idea of giving from the heart and set off on a picture-postcard tour of Christmas celebrations around the world before returning home to revel in peaceful days of gratitude and reflection.

Traditions of Christmas brings together all the wonder and enchantment this heartwarming season evokes, offering inspiration for all the Christmases to come.

Greeting the SEASON

*Long before the stockings are hung or the first
gift is opened, the gracious spirit of Christmas begins
at a welcoming front door. The long-observed custom
of dressing the entryway with evergreen wreaths and
garlands issues a cordial invitation for guests to
come in and celebrate the season.*

A WARM WELCOME

Festoons of fresh greenery, threaded with yards of silky ribbon and bearing generous clusters of bright berries, form festive Yuletide greetings to all who enter these inviting abodes.

Opposite: Rather than confining door décor to the exterior, this artistic homeowner painted avian-themed designs on the panels, which are trimmed in gold leaf. While beautiful on its own, the entrance is enhanced for the holidays with a trio of wreaths and a gracefully draped garland entwined with blue velvet ribbon. This page, above, left to right: Tendrils of red streamers, unfurling from bows, lend a cheerful contrast to evergreen garlands ascending the banister, while kindred ribbons perform a similar role in an outdoor scene, set amid classic wrought ironwork.

Opposite: Pairing rich gold ribbon with fresh cedar and magnolia perfectly complements the dark wood of the double-door entrance to create a genteel effect. This page: A striking tricolor entryway, punctuated with a crimson door, needs only a wreath and garland to be holiday ready.

SENDING LOVE

A heartfelt holiday message, delivered by hand or by post, is sent with best wishes and received with great joy. These missives bring additional delight when displayed throughout the home.

Yuletide greeting cards come in a wide assortment of designs, from quaint reproductions that resemble those from Victorian times to the current trend of family portraits. There are many creative ways to display them, whether lined up on the mantel, tucked into a basket, or clipped to branches of the Christmas tree. One creative homeowner brought holiday charm into her guest room by draping a garland across the antique headboard, attaching a handful of pretty cards from ribbons, and mixing festive red accents with luxurious lace bedding.

FESTIVE FINERY

Mother Nature lends a hand to Christmas décor when colorful fruits, flowers, berries, and pine cones are styled alongside the fresh greenery at the heart of holiday displays.

Once considered a rare wintertime find, citrus fruits add a welcome splash of color to holiday decorations, both indoors and out. Opposite: Mini trees, made by attaching lemons and oranges to foam cones, pair with roses on the mantel, while a bowl of clementines—stems and leaves intact—brings zest to the table. This page: As striking as it is simple, a shapely glass vase, filled with a merry mix of oranges and seeded eucalyptus, makes an eye-catching centerpiece.

Opposite: Reminiscent of the omnipresent holiday displays found in Colonial Williamsburg, this oversized wreath is made by wiring magnolia leaves and sprigs of fresh balsam fir to a circular form, then filling in with both red and green apples and a mix of pine cones in a variety of sizes. This page, above, left to right: Decorating the mailbox at Christmastime has become a visual expression of Yuletide cheer, whether it is jingle bells and pine cones tucked amid a swag of evergreens or an exuberant blend of solid and variegated greenery caught up with a red bow.

Opposite: A simple boxwood wreath lends a gracious note to a gilt setting. This page, clockwise from top left: Even the tiniest vignettes, tucked here and there about the home, bring considerable measures of Christmas spirit to interiors—a bouquet of white roses in a silver vase nestled within a tea set, mini circlets bearing a sweet greeting, a beribboned swag of pine tied to a sconce. Petite kumquats and mandarin oranges bestow their bright colors on a wreath, while a tin bucket brimming with cedar and berries offers a cheerful touch, and classic flowers, such as orchids, bring an air of elegant sophistication to any holiday setting. Gleaming pomegranates look almost like ornaments beside a lush arrangement of roses and peonies.

Trimming the
EVERGREEN

As the true centerpiece of holiday decorations, the Christmas tree is both the shining symbol of Yuletide celebrations and the perfect outlet for expressing personality and sentiment. From traditional trimmings of red and green to the breathtaking splendor of silver and gold, these humble branches are easily elevated to star status.

Opposite: Nine thousand glittering lights bring this shimmering tree to life, and the enchantment is doubled when reflected in the foyer's gilded mirror. This page: A chandelier crown tops a graceful fir bedecked with strands of crystal beading and a treasure trove of ornaments.

Opposite: Sweet bouquets of miniature roses, tucked in upturned crystal bells, offer lovely botanical touches to a tree, below left, while ornaments trimmed in gold catch and reflect the twinkling lights, above right. Above left and this page: Traditional red and green is elevated to glamorous heights with a generous measure of metallic touches. This tree features a trio of D. Stevens wired ribbon streamers—rich red, white with gold embellishment, and tartan plaid—which cascades in gentle curves from the top. Ornaments in the style of antique Victorian Christmas cards add a nostalgic component, while Caspari wrapping papers echo the patterns and hues of the garlands.

Stitched together with the silken thread of elegance, the decorative elements that sparkle on a fresh fir tree bring an air of gilded glamour to this Christmas scene. Countless strands of fairy lights lend brilliance, making every ornament shine even brighter. Dainty cherubs clasp white rose nosegays as they make their way among the boughs to the star on top.

With interiors this opulent, only a tree of equal stature will do. A love for Old-World style, in all its golden glory, inspired the decorations, including multiple strands of lights, as well as clip-on candles reminiscent of the authentic articles, which first graced trees in sixteenth-century Germany. Satiny ribbons, echoing the carved curlicues of the plaster-relief ornamentation on the ceiling, flow down like gilded waterfalls from a beautifully gowned angel, who presides over the Yuletide festivities from her treetop post. Framed portraits of the homeowner's beloved relatives and cherished pets are interspersed with a collection of delicate metallic ornaments, from simple orbs to more fanciful shapes.

THE CHRISTMAS TREE

TEXT MARGARET HENDLEY

As a child, two things marked the beginning of Christmas to me. First was the arrival of my aunt Margaret, who would travel by train from New York City a day or two before Christmas. My father—typically joined by my older sister, Judy, and me—would make the forty-mile drive from our small town in Connecticut to pick her up.

The second event was the decorating of the tree. It was the custom in our family to do this on Christmas Eve, and as soon as my sister and I grew beyond toddlerhood, we were allowed to participate: a responsibility we took very seriously. Dad's role in this process was to purchase the tree and, usually accompanied by some language unbefitting the festive season, erect it in the large bay window at the end of our long living room.

But the year I was seven, I awoke to a snowy Christmas Eve morning with a sore throat and looking generally peaked, so that my mother determined I could not participate in the ritual of meeting my aunt, and much to my disappointment, Judy and Dad left without me. Before they returned home, I felt even worse and was put to bed with the hope that some extra rest would restore my normally robust health.

By early evening, however, it was obvious that I was quite ill. There was no twenty-four-hour clinic or hospital in town. There was, however, our family doctor, who lived about a half mile away at the bottom of the steep hill on which we lived. My worried mother called Dr. Caney, and he agreed to come immediately. However, when he stepped outside his door on that stormy night, he decided that his skis, rather than his car, were a more trustworthy mode of transport. Strapping his medical bag to his back, he headed up the hill, arriving a bit winded but ready to diagnose his feverish patient as suffering from acute tonsillitis. He administered some medicine and advised my parents that I avoid all excitement and remain in bed for the next forty-eight hours.

I really don't remember any part of that evening, but it is all part of the family lore. I am sure that my grateful and hospitable parents offered the good doctor some liquid refreshment before he left. I hope he enjoyed his downhill ski home, back to his own family and fireside. The next morning, I was much too sick to go to church or even come downstairs to open my presents. I drifted in and out of sleep all day, ignoring even the one or two gifts my big sister snuck to my bedside.

That evening, however, just before dinner was served, my father came upstairs to see me. And this part I remember very well. I was so worried that the tree could not possibly have been decorated without my help, that I finally woke up and croaked, "The tree! The tree!" Ignoring my mother's admonitions that I must stay in bed, my father picked me up, blankets and all, and carried me downstairs to the living room. He laid me on the sofa, which faced the beautifully decorated evergreen. Then he walked around, turning off all the lamps in the room, leaving it illuminated only by the twinkling lights.

I lay there gazing at its beauty while the rest of my family went into the dining room across the hall for dinner. I lay there listening to their happy voices while I smelled the pine, that most wonderful of Christmas fragrances. I lay there alone in the almost-dark, fully absorbed in the beauty of the season.

I am sure that when I had recovered sufficiently, I finally opened my presents with my usual greedy enthusiasm. But I never forgot that special Christmas. Even now, when my attempts to create the perfect Christmas for my loved ones often need the restraining voice of my husband, who states, "Enough already!" to my plans to purchase just one more gift or do just one more thing in this too-crowded season, I remember that evening. And at least once each December, I take a few precious moments to sit alone in our darkened living room, illumined only by the lights of our Christmas tree, and in the quiet, remember the voices of those I love who are all now silenced, while I ponder the mystery and wonder of this most blessed of celebrations.

Flocked to snowy perfection, this brimful evergreen celebrates the holidays with joyful elegance. Shades of gold and silver blend beautifully with those of ivory and white. Faux roses mingle with an array of pretty baubles and whimsical ornaments, while strings of pearls add a classically feminine note to the display.

When the tenth anniversary of the revival of our beloved *Victoria* magazine coincided with Christmastime, there was no better way to celebrate the milestone than with a resplendent holiday fête. A dreamy palette of blush, gold, and ivory lent both glamour and grandeur to the occasion, with the chosen hues appearing in all aspects of the setting, from dinnerware and florals to the very Champagne sipped to salute a decade of bliss. Dusted with a frosting of faux snow, the tree was dressed in bows and ball ornaments in pearlescent shades of cream and gold, while glimmering strands of lights illuminated the scene—a dazzling touch of éclat for this momentous occasion.

Posies of white mini roses and clusters of ivory hypericum berries mingle amid glistening boughs, where soft blue accents punctuate a bevy of alabaster ornaments trimmed in gold. Miniature replicas of violins bestow a personal touch for a family to whom music is an important interest. In lieu of the traditional star, this evergreen wears a lovely crown of ribbons and roses.

"FRESHLY CUT CHRISTMAS TREES SMELLING OF STARS AND SNOW AND PINE RESIN— INHALE DEEPLY, AND FILL YOUR SOUL WITH WINTRY NIGHT."

—John Geddes

As one of the world's most beloved Yuletide tales, *The Nutcracker* is forever woven into the fabric of Christmastime celebrations. Taking inspiration from the classic "fairy ballet" that dates to 1892—and from the magical realm of childhood imagination—this fabulous fir brims with ornaments depicting tiny nutcrackers and other notable characters from the story, along with an assemblage of gilded baubles and bouquets of crimson roses. At the base of the tree, treasured teddy bears have seats of honor among the brightly colored packages, and dolls dressed in their holiday finery await the excitement of Christmas morn.

Decking the HALLS

Herald the annual arrival of Christmastime by adorning interiors in classic keepsakes and glittering boughs. Whether honoring the traditional palette of red and green or incorporating more contemporary shades, decorative tokens set the tone for celebration throughout the home, making way for a season brimming with festivity and hope.

THE GRANDEUR OF GOLD

A home richly timeworn with burnished patina and bejeweled with ornaments exults in the spirit of the season.

Aureate splendor creates infinite potential for holiday magic in rooms graced with lavish style and classic design. Amid such sumptuous surrounds, festive flourishes dress the halls for Yuletide. Simple additions to the décor, such as placing a Christmas angel wrapped in a wintry frock atop a table, befit the Old-World ambiance of this home.

Natural adornments lend fragrant woodland elements to the scene. A garland of golden ribbon intertwined with fresh evergreen branches makes a bold statement atop an elegantly curved wrought-iron banister, while festoons of greenery laced with tiny lights, ribbon, and gilded accents adorn the sitting room fireplace.

Magnificent in scale and proportion, a tree decorated with hundreds of lights and sparkling ornaments reflects the extraordinary opulence of this majestic boudoir. A picture-perfect complement to the room's regal four-poster bed, the awe-inspiring evergreen creates heartwarming enchantment when set aglow in the evening hours.

IN GRAND VICTORIAN SPIRIT

Drawn to nineteenth-century decorative arts, a couple tasked designer Kathy Ellis with conveying the sumptuousness of that era in their interiors. At Yuletide, the pair's 1923 charmer brims with traditional holiday elegance.

An exuberant garland, with its scrolling ribbons, vintage ornaments, and other adornments, offers a fitting complement to the richly hued upholstery and rug.

A Lenox China Jewels Nativity holds pride of place in the living room. Echoing the pearlescent glow of ivory bone china, alabaster streamers cascade from bows nestled atop a 9-foot-tall Fraser fir. A decorative angel tops the tree, and another pair rests on a nearby credenza.

Left and above: A cherished pattern for the family's Christmas entertaining, Noritake Royal Hunt sets a festive mood with its plaid band, painted woodland motifs, and gilded edges. Opposite: For a sterling centerpiece, they favor a circa 1860 silver tureen from Scotland distinguished by a coat of arms, the hallmark of its original owners.

Opposite: Purchased from a local florist, fresh-cut cedar boughs bring natural beauty. This page: An English secretary showcases an array of prized nutcrackers from Steinbach and other German makers. One of the homeowners has collected the wooden figures for more than thirty years.

"MY CLIENTS LOVE ANTIQUES FROM THE VICTORIAN PERIOD AND THE HISTORY BEHIND THEM."
—Kathy Ellis

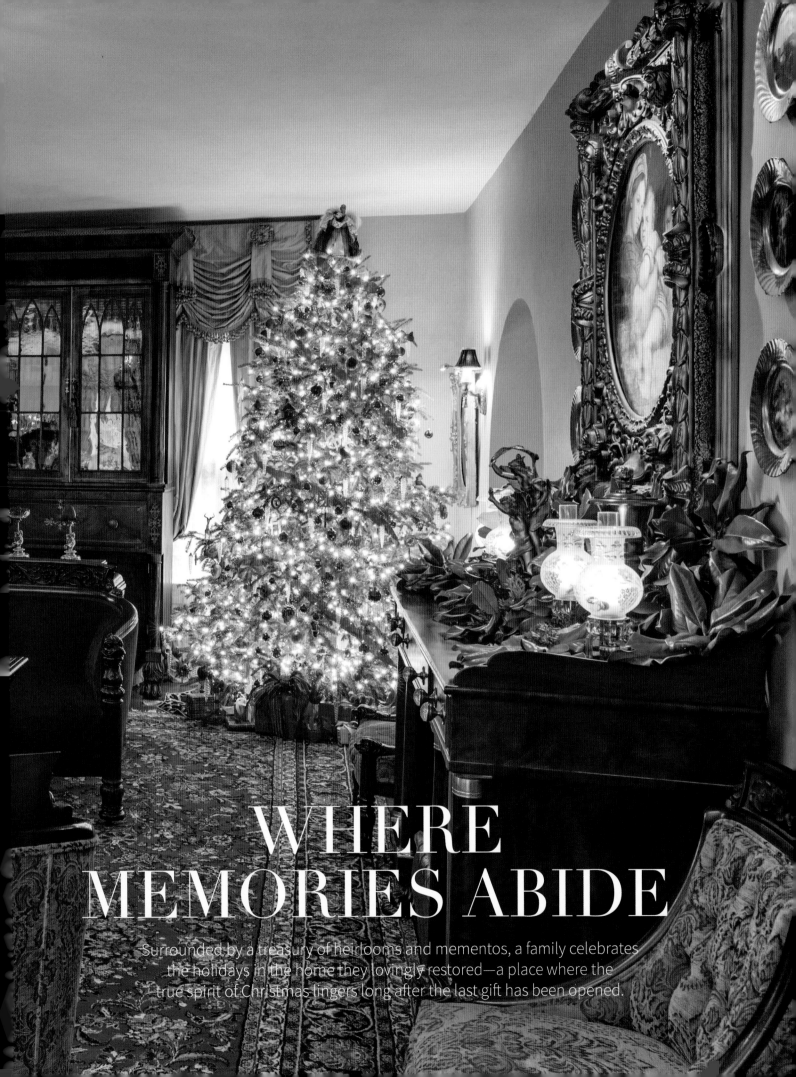

WHERE
MEMORIES ABIDE

Surrounded by a treasury of heirlooms and mementos, a family celebrates
the holidays in the home they lovingly restored—a place where the
true spirit of Christmas lingers long after the last gift has been opened.

Opposite: Every year, the Britts gather around their rare, mid-nineteenth-century triple-pedestal mahogany table for Christmas dinner. This page, above right: Nineteenth-century French china features hand-painted scenes inspired by Angelica Kauffman's paintings and is complemented by antique hand-blown cranberry glass goblets in the classic Christian Dorflinger Renaissance pattern.

Huntsville, Alabama, residents Jennifer and Mitchell Britt spent years looking for a house in the city's downtown district before coming across a classic Georgian that won their hearts in 1981. "When we walked through the back door and I saw that staircase, I knew this was the home for us," says Jennifer. "The Adams-style mantel in the living room was icing on the cake."

As is often the case, the circa 1926 structure came with a few problems—no air conditioning, a noisy steam boiler, and a kitchen that hadn't been updated in sixty years. Fortunately, the couple looked past the "institutional green" paint and astronaut wallpaper—a nod to Huntsville's NASA connection—and envisioned the showplace it could be. They did most of the work themselves, and between this restoration and the one at their farm, which is highlighted on page 76, they've acquired quite an impressive skill set.

The Britts raised their two children here, and the home brims with a lifetime of heartfelt memories, especially those made during the holidays, when four generations gather in the dining room or enjoy Grandmother's homemade cream rolls in the breakfast room. Vintage glass ornaments and other sentimental adornments trim two fresh-cut trees, while Yuletide collections rest amid a thoughtfully curated assemblage of antiques, such as a brass-inlaid secretary once owned by Mary Todd Lincoln's sister, Elodie Todd Dawson.

Inspired many years ago by a family trip to Colonial Williamsburg, the entrance's decoration is a true labor of love. Hundreds of magnolia leaves, culled from their farm, fan out around the door, with the largest ones at the base and the smallest covering the fan light above. Their son, Lance, adds the fruit—more than a hundred apples, two lemons, and one pineapple—while his mother crafts the fresh cranberry wreath. "Many neighbors tell us it isn't Christmas until our door is decorated each year," says Mitchell.

With the holidays on their doorstep, the Britts cheerfully start preparing their beloved residence for the festivities. "We have had some very happy years in this home," says Jennifer. "I love this place. I can't imagine life without it."

"THE HOUSE IS JUST FULL OF IRREPLACEABLE MEMORIES ... YEARS OF HAPPINESS."
—Jennifer Britt

Opposite: A fresh evergreen garland, woven with exquisite hand-beaded ribbon, drapes from the staircase balustrade; a sixteenth-century Belgian tapestry hangs at the landing. This page: A nineteenth-century English Copeland Spode tea set in the Fleur de Lis pattern is part of Jennifer's extensive collection of blue-and-white dinnerware.

Above left: The guest room holds an early-nineteenth-century American Empire acanthus-carved four-poster. Opposite: A late-eighteenth-century French Tambour embroidery stand rests at the foot of the primary bedroom's seventeenth-century English Jacobean oak tester bed, which features hand-carved linen-fold panels.

GREETINGS FROM MAGNOLIA GLEN

By staying true to the authentic character of this lovingly restored historic home, a Southern family celebrates the most jubilant time of year amid period-perfect furnishings and cherished collections.

In search of a second home with ample land for hunting, Jennifer and Mitchell Britt came across a circa 1833 Carolina cottage, complete with a classic dogtrot hallway and a dedicated chapel room, originally built for Juliet and Stephen Palmer. It had been vacant for years, but Jennifer could see beyond the layers of peeling paint to the charm beneath. Though her husband claimed "no power on this earth" would make him purchase the place, he had a change of heart, and the next morning, the papers were signed.

The couple spent more than two decades painstakingly restoring the house they named Magnolia Glen, a nod to the 400-year-old tree whose roots have formed a natural bridge across a creek on the property. They did most of the work themselves, with Jennifer, a French hand-sewing and textile specialist, stitching bespoke draperies and bed coverings, using techniques common in the mid-nineteenth century.

The Britts' son, Lance, owner of The Brittany House Antiques at Oak Hill, has lived here for the past ten years. Christmas is always a grand occasion. The family revived a tradition from the residence's earlier days with an annual open house on the first Saturday in December—an event the whole community looks forward to. Jennifer prepares a tantalizing array of scrumptious desserts, including her grandmother's unforgettable jam cake.

"Because we use a live cedar tree and greenery from the grounds of Magnolia Glen, we wait until the first week of December to decorate," explains Lance. "It typically takes five full days to decorate the tree and the house." The rooms ring with a regal holiday spirit, with garlands mingling ivy, cedar, and boxwood, a centerpiece made from dozens of fresh lemons holding sway in the dining room, and a tree laden with vintage Victorian ornaments reigning in the parlor.

Although it truly shines at Christmastime, every single day spent at this special place is precious in Lance's eyes. "It has been a true joy to watch my parents save Magnolia Glen and bring it back to life," he relates. "I feel blessed to have the opportunity to care for it and share it with others."

Above left: Nineteenth-century French Limoges china bears the Britt family monogram. Opposite: Brightening the dining room with the fresh appeal of citrus, a lemon topiary completes this tableau.

Opposite: An 11-foot, fresh-cut cedar sparkles in the formal parlor. This page, above left: Lance Britt's collection of antique and vintage toys nestles under the tree. A cast-iron train, a wagon, and blocks from his childhood are joined by Steiff bears, a tin carousel, and a late-nineteenth-century stereoscope. Above right: Sunburst window treatments adorn the windows of the chapel.

Clockwise from above right: An eighteenth-century copy of George Washington's writings and Victorian Christmas cards are among the treasures atop a nineteenth-century Philadelphia secretary in the "Preacher's Room." A circa 1821 American Federal mirror reflects antique inlaid lap desks atop an American Empire linen press, while a hand-quilted stocking hangs beneath antique greetings. In the entry, a hand-painted Sèvres epergne brims with white roses, cedar, and magnolia leaves. Festoons of greenery invite passersby to gather around for a rousing interlude of singing Christmas carols. Atop an American Empire mahogany dessert server, an antique cut-glass punch bowl with matching cups holds a holiday favorite, wassail.

"WHAT IS CHRISTMAS? IT IS TENDERNESS FOR THE PAST, COURAGE FOR THE PRESENT, HOPE FOR THE FUTURE."
—Agnes M. Pharo

THE SOFTER SIDE OF WINTER

A neutral palette, enlivened with just the subtlest hints of color, proves that Christmas trimmings can be understated and elegant while still capturing the joie de vivre of the season.

Opposite: An ivory-hued Nativity scene mimics the intricately carved details of the table. This page: Tinted mercury glass ornaments lend vintage charm to a simple yet lovely display.

Clockwise from above left: Burnished metallic ornaments nestle amid feathery fronds, and lacy, textured dinnerware in a mix of patterns forms the enchanting foundation for a wintertime setting. Intriguing scrolls of vintage sheet music, wrapped in snippets of ribbon, sit beside exquisitely wrapped presents. Opposite: A silver candelabrum brings a sophisticated element to the dessert table—a monochromatic scheme that imparts a peaceful ambiance throughout the home.

Opposite: A soupçon of Yuletide spirit appears in the primary suite, where greenery garnishes the bed posters and a trio of packages awaits on the bench. This page, clockwise from above: Fresh-cut ivory roses mirror the carved beauties atop the vanity jar lid, while an assemblage of ornaments repeats colors in the painting above. A lace dressing gown adds a luxurious touch.

Opposite: Shades of white hold sway over this holiday table; turquoise accents and fresh greenery offer dashes of color. This page: Champagne flutes elevate the level of sophistication, above left, while antique brooches clipped onto seafoam-green ribbon become one-of-a-kind napkin rings, above right.

HEAVEN & NATURE SING

The joyous birth of the Christ child
and a beautiful sylvan setting lend inspiration
for holiday decorations that enhance
a home's breathtaking interiors and set
the scene for heartfelt celebrations.

Opposite: *When Snow Yields to Spring*, a painting by American
traditionalist G. Harvey, takes pride of place in the library, where soaring
ceilings lend a sense of drama. An evergreen tree is trimmed with
ornaments that offer an expression of the homeowners' faith.

Opposite: The Morrisons' cozy keeping room, just off the kitchen, features a carved Gothic-style ceiling that echoes the flying buttress supports seen in European cathedrals. Kathy Ellis creates the indoor swags by wiring several different garlands together and accenting with floral picks.

Cindy and Tim Morrison have lived in myriad houses from coast to coast during their 45-year marriage, but their move to a tranquil and secluded Southern community in 2013 proved to be "the most beautiful, the most peaceful place" they'd ever lived. When they decided they wanted more space for their expanding family, which now includes eleven grandchildren, the couple found just what they needed in the same serene neighborhood: an impressive residence designed in the Châteauesque style of the Biltmore Estate.

Since the dwelling boasts towering ceilings, breathtaking architectural details, and an abundance of natural light, Cindy worked with her trusted designer, Kathy Ellis, who also styled the interiors on page 60, to ensure the furnishings complemented these majestic features. As is often the case with longtime collaborators, Kathy understood Cindy's vision for her home. The marriage of aesthetics and comfort results in the perfect gathering place for the Morrison clan—and that is never more evident than during the Yuletide season.

For many years, Kathy has also embraced the task of decorating Cindy's quarters for the holidays—an effort that takes the designer and her crew about five days to complete. The sophisticated cream-and-gold palette is in keeping with the manor's elegant presence, and she honors the property's forested surroundings with bountiful swags and a bevy of trees.

Threads of family and faith are intertwined in all that Cindy does. "I wanted the library tree to tell the story of salvation, from Jesus's birth to the resurrection," she explains. Since Christmas is a time for wishes, hers came true, and this tree, along with one covered stand-to-star in heirloom and handmade ornaments and another reflecting a nature theme, are shining highlights of the Morrison family's annual celebrations in this grand and gracious home.

The Morrisons place a special children's tree in the sitting area of the upstairs hall. Brimming with collected keepsakes and sentimental ornaments made by tiny hands, it is also adorned with garlands of hand-strung popcorn, cranberries, and dried apple and orange slices—a task Cindy accomplishes with help from her grandchildren. Above: Cathedral-style windows welcome in natural sunlight by day, while twin chandeliers, strategically placed so they do not block the view to the grand fireplace, ensure the dining room is perfectly lit for evening meals. The table showcases dinnerware in the Johnson Brothers classic Victorian Christmas pattern.

"TO CHERISH PEACE AND GOODWILL, TO BE PLENTEOUS IN MERCY, IS TO HAVE THE REAL SPIRIT OF CHRISTMAS."

—Calvin Coolidge

Demonstrating that not all adornments need to
the exuberant to be impactful, many spaces in the
Morrisons' home benefit from thoughtfully placed yet
simple decorations. Opposite: Perhaps even more
charming due to its petite stature, a tabletop tree adds
a nostalgic touch to a bedroom perfectly suited to
welcoming grandchildren. This page, above: Wreaths
highlight the architectural beauty of a bedside mirror
and nearby windows.

Collecting
TREASURES

Carefully wrapped in tissue paper and reverently brought out each year, cherished mementos of Christmases past hold a prized position among our holiday decorations. Whether passed down through the family tree or gathered by a single generation, these Yuletide favorites have earned a special place of safekeeping in our hearts and homes.

UPON THE
BOUGH

Whether fashioned by tiny hands or master artisans, each ornament proudly displays its value when hung upon an evergreen branch. These silvered versions, gleaming beneath vibrant hues and sparkling glitter, hold a special place in the memories of collectors who grew up arranging them on the tree.

Two days before the Christmas of 1848, *The Illustrated London News* featured an engraving of Queen Victoria, Prince Albert, and five of their children standing around a tabletop tree bedecked in sweets, candles, and decorations from the prince's native Germany. Upon seeing this picture-perfect holiday celebration, the English-speaking world began to embrace the tradition of dotting their branches with glass globes.

The original *kugels*, a German word meaning "sphere," were invented in the town of Lauscha, known for its glassmaking since the late sixteenth century. Here, smiths used a metal pipe and various moulds to blow the material into round balls and eventually hollow figures. To create a lustrous finish, the inside was silvered by a special liquid coating. At first, mercury was tried, but it did not adhere well, so the ingredient was quickly abandoned. Nevertheless, the products beautified by this process are often called "mercury glass."

German glassblowers monopolized the industry for many years, exporting the adornments to America, where they were sold at five-and-dime stores. The market changed drastically at the start of World War II, but thanks to German immigrant Max Eckardt, the States would still have their cherished baubles. The owner of a glassblowing enterprise, Max feared his U.S. supply of German ornaments would be compromised due to the war, so he moved his business to the land of opportunity and founded Shiny Brite in 1937, a company producing unique designs treasured by households throughout the mid-twentieth century.

Today, Christmas lovers delight in discovering ornaments by Shiny Brite and other makers from this period at antiques shops and flea markets. Many of the pieces in our vignettes are by this beloved manufacturer—identified most easily by their textured silver cap and colorful patterns. They remind collectors of their childhood, of a simpler and more innocent time, and of the Yuletide spirit embodied by Queen Victoria and her family so long ago.

Reproduction Shiny Brite ornaments are still produced today by Christopher Radko, mimicking the same vibrantly colored and uniquely shaped jewels collectors remember from childhood. Opposite: Similar pieces by other 1950s manufacturers hang from a tinsel tree.

VESTIGES OF A SACRED PAST

For one couple, strolling the byways of Europe—and especially exploring its storied cathedrals—sparked an interest in collecting religious artifacts. Cherished finds evoke memories of the journeys that led to each discovery.

Opposite: Before framing, this fragment of Flemish tapestry was taken to a preservationist, who rewove portions. This page, above: A seventeenth-century oak panel featuring English kings offers a stately backdrop for a contemporary snow village.

It was a Sunday afternoon in 1992 when interior designer Jan Cash and her husband, Stan, found their most beloved objet d'art. The pair had just arrived in Munich for a tour of Germany and, eager to become oriented, set out to walk the quiet streets. Without a map to guide them or an itinerary to limit their wanderings, the outing took on a dreamlike quality as the pair became immersed in the ancient city's beauty.

As they passed an antiques shop, an exquisite angel displayed in the window took Jan's breath away. She wanted to purchase it, but the store was closed, and she doubted they would ever stumble upon the location again. To her relief, Stan led her back the next morning, and a kindly shopkeeper explained that the hand-carved wooden figure had been salvaged from a demolished church outside of town. He offered to mail the piece to their home in the United States.

Although the shipping estimate was three weeks, the package did not arrive for three months. In fact, Jan had nearly given up hope when the call came to pick it up. In one last twist, the wrong box was given to the Cashes before the customs agent double-checked the labels and finally placed the seventeenth-century treasure in their care.

The German angel takes pride of place in a trove of antiques that encompasses religious artwork from around the world. Removed from their original context, these objects of devotion continue to intrigue collectors, whether for their subject matter, age, or quality. Paintings and tapestries portray ethereal themes, folk art statuettes called *santos* depict noted saints, and other relics call to mind sacred customs from bygone eras.

Pieces are often admired for the skill and dedication evinced through their creation, as well as for the fine materials used. Many architectural fragments, for example, reflect a level of workmanship seldom found in the modern age. Jan points out the Gothic detail on a carving reclaimed from a house of worship in England. Probably built in the 1700s to grace an altar or choir loft, the oak tracery pattern incorporates a classic quatrefoil motif.

Although Jan displays her prized heirlooms throughout the year, thoughtfully curated vignettes take on a unique splendor at Christmastime. Bits of greenery add winter charm, and gilded accents seem to glow even brighter amid the lights of the season.

Holiday adornments include, clockwise from above left, a grouping of reproduction Belsnickles set before an oak tracery panel, a boxwood wreath highlighting the Cashes' beloved German angel, and candles and greenery added to a walnut bookcase.

NUTCRACKER SUITE

From their humble beginnings as fanciful yet practical tools to the beloved Christmas accessories they've become, these charming keepsakes bring a whimsical touch to Yuletide décor.

> *"THE NUTCRACKER SITS UNDER THE HOLIDAY TREE, A GUARDIAN OF CHILDHOOD STORIES."*
> —Vera Nazarian

For many, Tchaikovsky's ballet *The Nutcracker* was their first introduction to dancing wooden figures that resemble toy soldiers, but the history of these carved collectibles dates back centuries before the show's 1892 debut. Seventeenth-century German craftsmen sculpted similar models that often were seen as good luck symbols in their homeland. Eventually, the popularity of these miniature military men spread beyond Germany's borders, and somewhere along the way, they became associated with Christmas, a connection still celebrated today. Bernardaud's sophisticated Grenadiers dinnerware, shown opposite, is a classic example of the whimsical nutcracker's enduring association with the holiday.

Opposite: Nutcrackers come in many guises and sizes, though few actually do the job that their name suggests. While originally carved of hardwood, newer versions of these coveted collectibles may be made of other materials, such as resin. This page, clockwise from above: Tchaikovsky loosely based his ballet on E. T. A. Hoffmann's book *The Nutcracker and the Mouse King*—though he softened the story a bit for the stage. Children and adults alike enjoy attending local performances of the perennial favorite production, with young ballerinas vying for the coveted role of Clara. Talented California-based gingerbread artist Teri Pringle Wood has garnered an enthusiastic following on Instagram with her detailed cookie creations. Here, her white-bearded treats mingle with pearl-adorned snowflake confections.

STERLING KEEPSAKES

Silver bells and porcelain acorns, tartan ribbons and frosted garlands, clip-on candles reminiscent of those in the centuries-old German tradition—the beautifully decorated tree of Editor-in-Chief Phyllis Hoffman DePiano sparkles with the brilliant hues of the season and a gallimaufry of sentimental collections.

Opposite: Phyllis's tree brims with treasured ornaments, including glass balls that her late mother painted in her daughter's favorite blue-and-white motif and the Reed & Barton Holly Bells that she and her husband, Neal, began collecting upon their marriage many years ago. This page: Resting atop a bow fashioned from tartan ribbon—another Christmas must—is Phyllis's "grandmother's bell," which commemorates the birth of her first grandchild.

*"A VOICE, A CHIME,
A CHANT SUBLIME
OF PEACE ON EARTH,
GOOD-WILL TO MEN!"*
—Henry Wadsworth Longfellow

Illuminated by clip-on candles and strands of twinkling lights, one of the silver treasures in Phyllis and Neal's collection shines alongside tartan-plaid ribbons, glittering garlands, and silk amaryllis blossoms tucked amid the boughs of the fresh fir. Every Christmas, Reed & Barton releases its annual Holly Bell ornament. Since the DePianos were married in a cozy "tree-light" ceremony just before the holiday, they add a bell each year to celebrate their anniversary while reminiscing about the sacred vows they exchanged before family and friends. In addition to brightening the evergreen, these baubles may adorn a wreath or mantel garland or be tied to a special gift.

This page and opposite: The DePianos are also drawn to acorn-themed items, such as these porcelain pretties, nestled among silver bells in an antique bride's basket that Phyllis received as a gift. The couple spent their honeymoon at the Biltmore Estate, where the acorn motif abounds. "They symbolize strength and growth," says Phyllis, "and we decided that would be a good theme for our marriage."

Entertaining with JOY

With the tree trimmed and interiors all aglow with the splendor of the holidays, the time is right for opening the door wide in welcome to all who come to call during this wonderful time of year. Recipes from the Victoria test kitchens ensure that guests will be treated to unforgettable fare, from a tea party savored with friends to Christmas Day brunch and dinner menus perfect for sharing with family.

SET TO SERVE

There is no better time than Christmas to invite people into your home. Inspired by the twinkle of lights, create a festive tablescape brimming with the sparkle of glorious gold and shining silver.

As the holidays draw near and the spirit of the season brings loved ones together, slip into a state of beauty and reverie surrounded by the soft glow of candles and the sumptuous comfort of serene surroundings. This time of year presents the perfect opportunity to add elegance to your décor with the finest china and linens from your treasured collections.

Antique china etched in an exquisite gold pattern is showcased atop a table cloaked in snowy white textiles and accented by graceful candelabras and a profusion of ivy. Snippets of greenery, holly, and roses tucked inside sterling goblets enhance each place setting, inviting guests to relax and delight in the simple loveliness of the moment.

Gilded crystal and the rich patina of silver cast their spell, while ornate touches and intricate details bring allure. The glimmer carries through to the focal point of Yuletide décor: the tree. A towering evergreen adorned with ribbon and gold ornaments complements the magical ambiance.

BLUE & WHITE TEATIME

Showcase transferware, along with other porcelain treasures in shades from brilliant cobalt to elegant navy, during a Christmas party that takes its style inspiration from a collection of beloved china. Vibrantly hued serving pieces present our menu to best effect, and festive adornments lend holiday ambiance to the occasion.

Clockwise from above right: Devonshire cream and orange marmalade accompany flaky Black Currant, Orange Peel, and Ginger Scones. Beribboned teacups, whether affixed to a package or tied to an evergreen branch, enhance the tableau. A gold-rimmed Sasha Nicholas platter draws the eye with a stately Couture Wreath monogram.

> ### "[BLUE AND WHITE] IS A BEAUTIFUL, CLASSIC PAIRING THAT THRIVES ON CONTRAST AND THE ASSOCIATIONS OF A LIFE WELL LIVED."
>
> —Mark D. Sikes

Opposite: Mixing patterns from different makers adds to the interest of an assemblage. Here, stately ciphers complement intricate borders, and pastoral scenes kindle the imagination. United by their enduring hue, new and antique finds come together gracefully to form a balanced composition where every motif can be appreciated fully. This page, left: Accents of green, including gleaming ornaments, lush ribbons, and shiny apples, enliven our palette of blue and white. Above: Rounds of English cucumber—sliced thin with a mandoline, folded into quarters, and arranged to create delicate ruffles—crown Cucumber and Smoked Salmon Canapés, golden triangles of toasted sourdough bread with tasty toppings tucked in silky layers of garlic and herbs cheese.

Above right: Horseradish gives a hint of spice to Lobster, Lemon, and Chive Phyllo Cups, a medley of seafood, citrus, and herb nestled in a crisp pastry shell. Opposite: Smoked Turkey with Cranberry Relish Tea Sandwiches lend seasonal charm to the savories course, while Curried Chicken Salad on Wheat Bread offers a taste of tradition welcomed any time of year.

Above left: Baked in petite portions, Chestnut Cakes incorporate the featured flavor in both batter and frosting. Edible gold leaf completes Dark Chocolate–Peppermint Truffles, bite-size candies that shelter minty filling and decadent ganache in a smooth coating of chocolate. Above right: Carefully sliced to reveal its intriguing checkerboard design, Amaretto and Almond Battenberg Cake boasts squares of sponge cake coated in jam and wrapped in vanilla fondant. Tinting half of the confection red instead of pink dresses the British specialty for Yuletide.

RECIPE INDEX

BLUE & WHITE TEATIME
Begins on page 130

Black Currant, Orange Peel, and Ginger Scones p.131
Makes 14

2¼ cups **all-purpose flour**
¼ cup **granulated sugar**
1 teaspoon **orange zest**
1 tablespoon **baking powder**
½ teaspoon ground **ginger**
¼ teaspoon **kosher salt**
5 tablespoons **unsalted butter**, cold and cubed
½ cup **candied orange slices**, finely chopped
½ cup **black currants**
¾ cup plus 1 tablespoon **buttermilk**, divided
1 large **egg**
Devonshire cream
Orange marmalade

1. Preheat oven to 400°. Line a rimmed baking sheet with parchment paper.
2. In a large bowl, stir together flour, sugar, orange zest, baking powder, ginger, and salt. Using a pastry blender or two forks, cut butter into flour mixture until it resembles coarse crumbs. Stir in candied orange and currants. Stir in ¾ cup buttermilk until a shaggy dough forms*.
3. Turn out dough onto a lightly floured surface, and knead until smooth. Roll to ¾-inch thickness. Using a 2-inch round fluted cutter, cut dough, rerolling scraps as needed. Place on prepared pan.
4. In a small bowl, whisk together egg and remaining 1 tablespoon buttermilk. Brush onto tops of scones.
5. Bake until a wooden pick inserted in centers comes out clean, about 14 minutes. Serve warm with Devonshire cream and marmalade.

*A shaggy dough is still lumpy yet cohesive and well blended.

Cucumber and Smoked Salmon Canapés p.132
Makes 15

5 slices **sourdough bread***, frozen
2 tablespoons **olive oil**
¼ teaspoon **kosher salt**
⅛ teaspoon ground **black pepper**
3 ounces **smoked salmon**, thinly sliced
¼ cup plus 2 tablespoons **garlic and herbs cheese**
1 **English cucumber**

1. Preheat oven to 400°. Line a rimmed baking sheet with parchment paper.
2. Using a 2½x2¼-inch triangle-shaped cutter, cut canapés from bread. Place on prepared pan. Brush olive oil on each side of canapés, and sprinkle with salt and pepper.
3. Bake until golden brown, about 12 minutes. Let cool completely on a wire rack.
4. Using a sharp knife or smaller triangle-shaped cutter, cut salmon slices.
5. Spread ½ teaspoon cheese on one side of each canapé; top with a triangle of salmon.
6. Fill a small piping bag with remaining cheese; pipe a small dot in center of each salmon triangle.
7. Using a mandoline on the thinnest setting, slice cucumber into rounds. Pat dry on paper towels. Fold cucumbers in half and then into quarters; place 3 slices, folded side down, on top of salmon, using piped cheese as adhesive. Cover with damp paper towels, and refrigerate in an airtight container until ready to serve.

*We used Pepperidge Farm.

Curried Chicken Salad on Wheat Bread p.134
Makes 18 finger sandwiches

¾ cup **Greek yogurt**
1 teaspoon **Jamaican-style curry powder**
1½ teaspoons fresh **mint**, finely chopped
½ teaspoon **kosher salt**
¼ teaspoon ground **black pepper**
2½ teaspoons fresh **lime juice**
8 ounces boneless, skinless **chicken breast**, cooked and shredded
18 slices **wheat bread***, frozen
Garnish: fresh **mint**

1. In a large bowl, whisk together yogurt, curry, mint, salt, pepper, and lime juice. Stir in chicken until fully coated in mixture.
2. Divide chicken salad among 12 bread slices (approximately 2 tablespoons per slice). Top 6 chicken salad–covered slices with remaining 6 chicken salad–covered slices; cover with remaining 6 bread slices.
3. Using a serrated knife with a sawing motion, remove crusts from bread and cut each sandwich into 3 finger sandwiches. Cover with damp paper towels, and refrigerate in an airtight container until ready to use.

*We used Dave's Killer Bread Thin-Sliced Good Seed.

Smoked Turkey with Cranberry Relish Tea Sandwiches p.134
Makes 12

12 slices **white bread***, frozen
½ pound **oven-roasted turkey breast**, thinly sliced
Cranberry Relish (recipe page 138)
Garnish: sliced fresh **cranberries, rosemary sprigs**

1. Using a 2-inch round cutter, cut 24 rounds

RECIPE INDEX

of bread and 12 rounds of turkey.

2. Top half of bread rounds with turkey and Cranberry Relish; cover with remaining half of bread rounds. Cover with damp paper towels, and refrigerate until ready to serve. Garnish with cranberry slices and rosemary, if desired.

We used Pepperidge Farm Original White Sandwich Bread.

Cranberry Relish
Makes approximately ½ cup

½ teaspoon **canola oil**
1 tablespoon finely chopped **red onion**
2 tablespoons **pineapple tidbits**
1½ teaspoons **pineapple juice***
1 teaspoon **lemon zest**
1½ teaspoons **lemon juice**
¼ teaspoon **cornstarch**
½ cup **whole-berry cranberry sauce***
⅛ teaspoon ground **cloves**
⅛ teaspoon ground **ginger**
⅛ teaspoon **salt**
⅛ teaspoon ground **black pepper**

1. In a medium saucepan, heat oil over medium heat. Add onion and cook until translucent, about 3 minutes.
2. In a small bowl, whisk together pineapple juice, lemon juice, and cornstarch.
3. To saucepan, add cranberry sauce, lemon zest, pineapples, cloves, ginger, salt, and pepper; stir to combine. Bring mixture to a boil, and stir in cornstarch mixture. Continue to boil, stirring frequently, until mixture registers 200° on an instant-read thermometer and has thickened, about 3 minutes.
4. Transfer to a heatproof bowl, and let cool on a wire rack, stirring occasionally. Refrigerate in an airtight container until ready to use.

We used pineapple juice reserved from pineapple tidbits and Ocean Spray Whole Berry Cranberry Sauce.

Lobster, Lemon, and Chive Phyllo Cups p.135
Makes 15

1 (1.19-ounce) box frozen **mini phyllo cups,** thawed
¼ cup **mayonnaise**
1 tablespoon **cream-style horseradish**
⅛ teaspoon **kosher salt**
⅛ teaspoon coarse **black pepper**
½ teaspoon **lemon zest**
½ teaspoon **lemon juice**
1½ teaspoons minced fresh **chives,** thinly chopped
8 ounces **cooked lobster-tail meat,** chopped
Garnish: minced fresh **chives, lemon curls**

1. Preheat oven to 400°. Line a rimmed baking sheet with parchment paper.
2. Place phyllo cups on prepared pan.
3. In a medium bowl, whisk together mayonnaise, horseradish, salt, pepper, lemon zest, lemon juice, and chives. Fold in lobster. Divide mixture among phyllo cups.
4. Bake until heated through, 8 to 10 minutes. Garnish with chives and lemon curls, if desired.

Chestnut Cakes p.136
Makes 24

½ cup **unsalted butter,** softened
1 cup **granulated sugar**
2 large **eggs,** room temperature
½ teaspoon **vanilla extract**
1 cup plus 2 tablespoons **all-purpose flour**
½ teaspoon **baking soda**
¼ teaspoon **kosher salt**
½ cup **buttermilk**
½ cup **roasted chestnuts*,** finely chopped
Chestnut Buttercream (recipe follows)
Garnish: fresh **mint, pomegranate arils**

1. Preheat oven to 350°. Place 2 (12-cavity) silicone moulds* on a rimmed baking sheet.
2. In the bowl of a stand mixer fitted with the paddle attachment, beat butter and sugar at medium speed until fluffy, 3 to 4 minutes, stopping to scrape down sides of bowl. Add eggs, one at a time, beating well after each addition. Beat in vanilla extract.
3. In a medium bowl, whisk together flour, baking soda, and salt. Reduce mixer speed to low. Gradually add flour mixture to butter mixture, alternately with buttermilk, beating until combined. Beat in chestnuts just until combined. Use a 2-teaspoon levered scoop to portion 2 scoops of batter into each cavity.
4. Bake until a wooden pick inserted in centers comes out clean, 15 to 18 minutes. Let cool in moulds for 10 minutes. Freeze for 20 minutes before removing from moulds.
5. Place Chestnut Buttercream in a piping bag fitted with a petal tip*. Pipe a zigzag design on tops of cakes. Garnish with mint and pomegranate arils, if desired.

We used Gefen Roasted & Peeled Whole Chestnuts, Celebrate It 12-Cavity Silicone Treat Molds, and a Wilton #102 decorating tip.

Chestnut Buttercream
Makes 3 cups

1 cup **unsalted butter,** softened
1 tablespoon **cocoa powder**
3 cups **confectioners' sugar**
1 (5.2 ounce) package **dry-roasted chestnuts,** finely ground
½ teaspoon **kosher salt**
3 tablespoons **heavy whipping cream**

1. In the bowl of a stand mixer fitted with the paddle attachment, beat butter at medium speed until creamy, about 3 minutes. Scrape down sides of bowl with a rubber spatula.
2. In a medium bowl, sift together cocoa powder, confectioners' sugar, ground chestnuts, and salt.

3. Reduce mixer speed to low, and gradually add sugar mixture, beating until combined after each addition. Add heavy cream and beat until smooth.

Dark Chocolate–Peppermint Truffles p.136
Makes 15

3 tablespoons plus ½ teaspoon **bittersweet chocolate chips***, finely chopped
2 tablespoons **heavy whipping cream**
½ cup plus 1 tablespoon **confectioners' sugar**
1 teaspoon **light corn syrup**
1 tablespoon **water**
⅛ teaspoon pure **peppermint extract**
¾ teaspoon **vegetable shortening**
1½ cups **dark chocolate melting wafers***
Garnish: crushed **peppermint candies**, edible **gold leaf**

1. Place chocolate chips in a medium bowl.
2. In a small saucepan, heat cream over medium heat, stirring frequently, until hot but not boiling. Pour over chocolate chips, stirring constantly until a smooth ganache forms. Press a piece of plastic wrap onto surface of ganache, and let cool.
3. In a medium bowl, beat confectioners' sugar, corn syrup, 1 tablespoon water, peppermint extract, and shortening until combined and smooth. If peppermint filling is too thick for piping, add water, 1 teaspoon at a time, and beat until desired texture is achieved. Transfer to an airtight container, and set aside.
4. In a large microwave-safe bowl, microwave chocolate wafers on medium in 30-second intervals, stirring between each, until chocolate is melted and smooth. Fill a 15-cavity silicone mould* with melted chocolate. Flip moulds over, and let excess chocolate drain into a bowl until outlines on bottom of mould are visible when mould is turned right side up. Let chocolate set slightly, and scrape off excess with a bench scraper or offset metal spatula. Let set completely, right side up.
5. Transfer ganache to a piping bag fitted with a small round tip*. Transfer peppermint filling to a piping bag fitted with a small round tip*. Fill chocolate shells half full with ganache. Pipe peppermint filling over ganache so shells are three-quarters full. Freeze for 10 minutes.

6. Reheat reserved melted chocolate until smooth, if necessary. Remove moulds from freezer, and fill to the brim with melted chocolate, scraping off excess with a bench scraper or offset metal spatula. Freeze for 10 minutes.
7. Remove truffles from moulds, and use a sharp paring knife to clean any rough edges. Store in an airtight container in a cool, dark place for up to 2 weeks. Garnish with peppermint candy and gold leaf, if desired.

*We used Ghirardelli Bittersweet 60% Cacao Baking Chips, Ghirardelli Dark Melting Wafers, a Lekue Silicone Chocolate Mold, and Wilton #7 decorating tips.

Amaretto and Almond Battenberg Cake p.136
Makes 2 (7½x3-inch) cakes

1 cup **unsalted butter**, softened
1 cup **granulated sugar**
2 large **eggs**
½ teaspoon **almond extract**
½ teaspoon **vanilla extract**
1¾ cups **all-purpose flour**
2 teaspoons **baking powder**
½ teaspoon **kosher salt**
2 tablespoons **cocoa powder**
1¼ teaspoons **red gel food coloring**
⅓ cup **amaretto-almond jam**
1 (24-ounce) box **white vanilla fondant***

1. Preheat oven to 350°. Spray an 8-inch square cake pan with cooking spray. Line pan with parchment paper, and spray again. Fold a sheet of foil 3 to 4 times to create a sturdy 8-inch-long, 1-inch-tall strip. Place in center of prepared pan to form a divider. Spray divider with cooking spray.
2. In the bowl of a stand mixer fitted with the paddle attachment, beat butter and sugar at medium speed until creamy, 3 to 4 minutes, stopping to scrape down sides of bowl. Add eggs, one at a time, beating just until combined after each addition. Beat in almond and vanilla extracts.
3. In a medium bowl, whisk together flour, baking powder, and salt.
4. With mixer at low speed, gradually add flour mixture to butter mixture, beating just until combined.
5. Pour half of batter into a separate medium bowl. Add cocoa and food coloring;

stir until mixture is evenly tinted.
6. Pour tinted batter into one side of prepared pan, and pour remaining batter into other side of pan.
7. Bake until a wooden pick inserted in centers comes out clean, 25 to 30 minutes. Let cool in pan for 10 minutes. Turn out cakes onto wire racks, and let cool completely.
8. Place cakes on a cutting surface. Using a serrated knife, trim off dark outer edges. Cut each cake lengthwise into 2 (7½x3-inch) rectangles, and then cut each rectangle into 2 (7½x1½-inch wide) pieces.
9. In a small saucepan, melt jam over low heat, stirring to loosen.
10. Using a pastry brush, coat tops and one side each of a white piece and a red piece with melted jam. Position these pieces next to one another so that the jam sides touch, and gently press together. Stack another red piece on top of bottom white piece, and brush interior side of red piece with jam. Place another white piece next to jam-coated red piece, and gently press together. Repeat with remaining cake pieces to form a second cake.
11. Knead and roll out fondant to ⅛-inch thickness. Use a sharp knife to cut a 14x8½-inch rectangle from fondant. Cover with plastic wrap. Knead and reroll fondant scraps, and cut a second rectangle.
12. Brush tops of each cake stack with melted jam. Wrap each cake with fondant, pressing and smoothing fondant to adhere to cake. Turn cake. Using kitchen shears, trim long edge of fondant, letting ends overlap slightly. Using fingers, press seam to seal. Gently roll cake over so seam is on bottom. Fold and tuck in ends of fondant to keep cake moist.
13. Using a straight edge, such as a plastic ruler, press down on fondant approximately every ½-inch to create angled stripes. Repeat, reversing direction of angled stripes, to create a diamond pattern.
14. Place cakes on cutting board, and wrap each securely in plastic wrap, making sure plastic is in contact with fondant to prevent it from drying out.
15. Just before serving, unwrap cake. Using a long serrated knife and a gentle sawing motion, trim ends and cut cake into ¾-inch-thick slices.

*We used Wilton Decorator Preferred White Fondant.

FESTIVE HOLIDAY BRUNCH

With the living room now a sea of ribbons and wrapping paper, a few culinary surprises still await discovery. Courtesy of a menu with elements that can be made ahead of time, tantalizing aromas lead the way to a banquet of mouthwatering fare.

Clockwise from above: Sample a mingling of sweet and savory perfect in any combination. Let us suggest English Muffins spread thickly with Maple-Cranberry Butter or Southern-style Buttery Biscuits topped with Brown Sugar and Honey–Glazed Ham or Ginger-Pear Preserves. Toast the celebration with flutes of our bubbly Blood Orange Mimosas.

Clockwise from above left: A garnish of capers and feathery dill offers the finishing touch to Crispy Potato Pancakes with Smoked Salmon and Dilled Sour Cream. Mixed Fruit Salad presents a medley of fruit on a bed of tender watercress. Atop a flaky crust, Sausage, Kale, and Roasted Red Pepper Tart boasts a thick filling of eggs and fontina cheese brimming with vegetables—a hearty dish that delivers satisfying flavor in every bite. Brunch culminates with Cream Cheese and Fresh Cherry Danish, a pastry worth lingering over with coffee.

RECIPE INDEX

FESTIVE HOLIDAY BRUNCH
Begins on page 140

Blood Orange Mimosas p.141
Makes approximately 12 servings

1 (11.15-ounce) can **blood orange sparkling fruit beverage, chilled***
6 ounces **blood orange juice**
1 (750-ml) **sparkling wine** or **Prosecco, chilled**
Garnish: **blood orange rind**

In Champagne flutes, pour approximately 1 ounce sparkling fruit beverage and ½ ounce blood orange juice. Fill glasses with sparkling wine or Prosecco. Garnish with orange rinds, if desired. Serve immediately.

We used Sanpellegrino Aranciata Rossa.

Buttery Biscuits p.141
Makes approximately 18

3½ cups **all-purpose flour***
1½ tablespoons **granulated sugar**
1 tablespoon **kosher salt**
1 tablespoon **baking powder**
½ teaspoon **baking soda**
1¼ cups cold **butter**, cubed
1 cup **whole buttermilk***
1 large **egg**, lightly beaten

1. Preheat oven to 425°. Line a baking sheet with parchment paper.
2. In a large bowl, whisk together flour, sugar, salt, baking powder, and baking soda. Using a pastry blender or 2 forks, cut in butter until mixture is crumbly. Gradually stir in buttermilk until a shaggy dough forms**.
3. Turn out dough onto a lightly floured surface. Pat dough into a rectangle, and cut into fourths. Stack fourths one on top of the other, and pat down into a rectangle again. Cut into fourths, stack fourths, and pat down into a rectangle 3 more times. Pat or roll dough to 1-inch thickness. Using a 2-inch round cutter dipped in flour, cut dough without twisting cutter, rerolling scraps as necessary. Place biscuits 2 inches apart on prepared pan.
4. Freeze until cold, about 10 minutes.
5. Brush with beaten egg. Bake until golden brown, about 15 minutes.

We used White Lily Flour, milled from soft red winter wheat for a light and fluffy biscuit. Additional buttermilk may be needed if a flour with higher protein content is used.

**A shaggy dough is still lumpy yet cohesive and well blended.*

English Muffins p.141
Makes 12

2½ cups **bread flour**
1 (0.25-ounce) package **rapid-rise instant yeast**
2 tablespoons **granulated sugar**
1 teaspoon **kosher salt**
1 teaspoon **baking powder**
1 tablespoon **butter**, softened
1 large **egg**
¾ cup warm **whole milk** (120° to 130°)
1 cup **cornmeal**, divided

1. In the bowl of a stand mixer fitted with the dough hook attachment, combine flour, yeast, sugar, salt, and baking powder. Beat in softened butter, egg, and warm milk at medium speed. Continue beating until dough is smooth and elastic, about 4 minutes.
2. Transfer dough to a lightly greased bowl, turning to grease top; cover with plastic wrap and refrigerate overnight.
3. Line a rimmed baking sheet with parchment paper; sprinkle a layer of cornmeal over pan. Sprinkle a layer of cornmeal over a large cast-iron skillet*.
4. Remove dough from refrigerator, and let stand until dough reaches room temperature, about 1½ hours.
5. On a lightly floured surface, divide dough into 12 portions. Shape each portion into a ball, and flatten into a disk. Place dough over cornmeal on prepared baking sheet, and sprinkle tops of dough with cornmeal. Lightly cover, and let stand in a warm, draft-free place (85°) for 20 minutes.
6. Preheat oven to 350°.
7. Place 6 dough rounds in skillet over cornmeal, and transfer skillet to stovetop. Heat over medium-low heat, allowing dough to come to temperature with pan. Cook, turning pan occasionally, until bottoms are golden brown, 5 to 6 minutes. Turn muffins and cook until golden brown, about 5 minutes more. Return muffins to prepared baking sheet. Remove skillet from heat, and allow to return to room temperature. Wipe skillet clean, and sprinkle remaining cornmeal over pan in a thin layer. Repeat procedure with remaining 6 muffins.
8. Transfer baking sheet to oven, and bake until an instant-read thermometer inserted in center of muffins registers 190°, about 10 minutes.

A griddle may be used in place of a cast-iron skillet, if desired.

RECIPE INDEX

Brown Sugar and Honey–Glazed Ham p.141

Makes 12 to 15 servings

½ cup firmly packed **brown sugar**
2 tablespoons **Dijon mustard**
1 tablespoon **honey**
2 teaspoons **orange zest**
1 (1-pound) boneless, sliced, fully cooked **ham**

1. Preheat oven to 325°.
2. In a small bowl, stir together brown sugar, mustard, honey, and orange zest.
3. In a 2-quart baking dish, place ham, flat side down. Spoon brown sugar mixture over ham; cover lightly with foil, and bake for 30 minutes. Uncover and bake 30 minutes more, basting ham with pan juices every 10 minutes. Cut into small pieces for serving.

Maple-Cranberry Butter p.141

Makes approximately 3 cups

1 (12-ounce) package fresh or frozen **cranberries**
½ cup **water**
¼ cup firmly packed **brown sugar**
¼ cup **maple syrup**
½ teaspoon ground **cinnamon**
1 cup **butter**, softened

1. In a medium saucepan, combine cranberries and ½ cup water. Bring to a boil over medium-high heat. Cook, stirring occasionally, until cranberries begin to burst.
2. Transfer cranberry mixture to the work bowl of a food processor. Add brown sugar, syrup, and cinnamon; process until mixture is combined. Add softened butter, and process until mixture is smooth.
3. Spoon butter mixture into a large bowl; cover and refrigerate for at least 4 hours and up to 3 days.

Ginger-Pear Preserves p.141

Makes approximately 3 cups

6 cups peeled, cored, and cubed **Bartlett pears**
3½ cups **granulated sugar**
½ cup **water**
¼ cup **pear juice**
2 teaspoons **lemon zest**
2 tablespoons fresh **lemon juice**
2 tablespoons chopped **crystallized ginger**
1 tablespoon finely chopped fresh **ginger**

1. In a large, heavy saucepan, combine pears, sugar, ½ cup water, pear juice, lemon zest, lemon juice, crystallized ginger, and fresh ginger. Bring to a boil over medium-high heat, stirring until sugar is dissolved. Reduce heat and simmer, stirring occasionally, until mixture is thickened, about 1 hour. Remove from heat and let cool to room temperature (preserves will continue to thicken as they cool).
2. Spoon preserves into a large bowl; cover and refrigerate for up to 1 week.

Mixed Fruit Salad with Pomegranate Vinaigrette p.142

Makes 8 to 10 servings

3 **Ruby Red grapefruit**, peeled and sectioned
3 **navel oranges**, peeled and sectioned
2 **Granny Smith apples**, thinly sliced
2 cups matchstick-cut **jicama**
1 (4.3-ounce) container **pomegranate arils**
2 (4-ounce) packages **watercress**
½ cup fresh **mint leaves**
Pomegranate Vinaigrette (recipe follows)

In a large bowl, toss grapefruit segments, orange segments, apples, and jicama. Add pomegranate arils, watercress, and mint leaves just before serving. Drizzle with desired amount of Pomegranate Vinaigrette.

Note: Citric acid in the grapefruit and oranges will keep the apples from browning, so the fruit can be tossed together, covered, and refrigerated for up to 1 day. Pomegranate arils tend to bleed, so they should be added just before serving.

Pomegranate Vinaigrette

Makes approximately ¾ cup

1½ cups **pomegranate juice**
⅓ cup **olive oil**
3 tablespoons **Champagne vinegar**
1½ teaspoons **honey**
1 teaspoon **Dijon mustard**
½ teaspoon **kosher salt**
¼ teaspoon ground **black pepper**

1. In a small saucepan, bring pomegranate juice to a boil over medium-high heat. Reduce heat and simmer until juice is reduced to ¼ cup.
2. Transfer pomegranate reduction to a medium bowl; let cool.
3. Whisk in olive oil, vinegar, honey, mustard, salt, and pepper until combined. Serve immediately, or cover and refrigerate for up to 3 days.

Crispy Potato Pancakes with Smoked Salmon and Dilled Sour Cream p.142

Makes approximately 36

3 pounds **russet potatoes**
1 **onion**, minced
1 cup **panko** (Japanese bread crumbs)
⅓ cup **all-purpose flour**
1 tablespoon **kosher salt**
2 large **eggs**, lightly beaten
8 tablespoons **butter**
8 tablespoons **vegetable oil**
1 (4-ounce) package **smoked salmon**
Dilled Sour Cream (recipe follows)
Garnish: **capers**, fresh **dill**

1. Peel potatoes. Using the large holes of a box grater, grate potatoes into a large bowl*. Add cold water to cover, and stir in onions. Cover and let stand at room temperature for 1 hour. Drain well.
2. Place potato mixture between layers of paper towels, squeezing to remove excess moisture*. In a large bowl, combine potato-onion mixture, bread crumbs, flour, and salt. Add beaten eggs, stirring to combine.
3. Line a large rimmed baking sheet with parchment, and set a wire cooling rack over parchment. Form potato mixture into 1½-inch rounds (about 2 tablespoonfuls), and place on parchment-lined pan.
4. In a large skillet, melt 2 tablespoons butter with 2 tablespoons oil over medium heat. Add one-fourth of potato rounds, and flatten with a spatula. Cook until bottoms are lightly browned, 3 to 4 minutes. Turn pancakes and cook until lightly browned, 3 to 4 minutes more. Transfer to prepared rack. Repeat procedure with remaining butter, oil, and potato rounds.
5. Cover pancakes and refrigerate for up to 3 days.
6. Preheat oven to 400°.
7. Bake until deep golden brown and crisp, 15 to 20 minutes. Serve warm or at room temperature topped with smoked salmon and Dilled Sour Cream. Garnish with capers and dill, if desired.

*Grated potatoes may be refrigerated over-night. The drier the potatoes are after being drained and wrapped in paper towels, the crispier the pancakes will be.

Dilled Sour Cream
Makes approximately 1 cup

1 (8-ounce) carton **sour cream**
2 tablespoons chopped fresh **dill**
1 tablespoon minced **capers**
1 teaspoon **lemon zest**
2 teaspoons fresh **lemon juice**

In a small bowl, stir together sour cream, dill, capers, lemon zest, and lemon juice. Cover and refrigerate for up to 3 days.

Sausage, Kale, and Roasted Red Pepper Tart p.142
Makes 1 (10-inch) tart

1 (14.1-oz) package refrigerated **piecrusts**
1 pound **ground Italian sausage**
½ **onion**, thinly sliced
1 bunch **cavolo nero***, stemmed and chopped
½ cup chopped **roasted red peppers**
2 cups shredded **fontina cheese**
6 large **eggs**
¾ cup **half-and-half**
½ teaspoon **crushed red pepper**

1. Preheat oven to 350°. Spray a 10-inch deep-dish tart pan with removable bottom with baking spray with flour.
2. On a lightly floured surface, unroll pie-crusts and stack one on top of the other. Roll crusts together into a 16-inch circle. Fit crusts into bottom and up sides of prepared pan. Line with parchment paper, and fill with pie weights.
3. Bake for 20 minutes. Carefully remove parchment and pie weights; set aside to let cool slightly.
4. In a large skillet, cook sausage and onion over medium heat until sausage is browned and crumbly. Gradually stir in cavolo nero, cooking until wilted. Stir in roasted peppers.
5. Spoon half of sausage mixture into prepared crust. Top with half of cheese; repeat layers.
6. In a medium bowl, whisk together eggs, half-and-half, and crushed pepper until combined. Pour over cheese in crust.
7. Place tart pan on a rimmed baking sheet. Bake until center is set, 45 to 60 minutes, covering tart with foil to prevent excess browning, if necessary. Serve warm or at room temperature.

*A member of the kale family used often in Italian cooking, this dark green, leafy heirloom is also known as Lacinato kale, Tuscan kale, and black kale.

Note: Crust may be baked up to 3 days before serving; sausage mixture may be cooked up to 3 days before assembly.

Cream Cheese and Fresh Cherry Danish p.142
Makes 2

5 cups fresh **cherries**, pitted and halved
⅔ cup plus 3 tablespoons **granulated sugar**, divided
¼ cup **cornstarch**
½ cup **water**
2 tablespoons fresh **lemon juice**
12 ounces **cream cheese**, softened
1 tablespoon **lemon zest**
2 large **eggs**, divided
1 (17.3-ounce) package frozen **puff pastry**, thawed
¼ cup **turbinado sugar**

1. In a large saucepan, combine cherries, ⅔ cup granulated sugar, cornstarch, ½ cup water, and lemon juice. Bring to a boil over medium-high heat, stirring frequently; reduce heat and simmer, stirring constantly, until mixture is very thick. Remove from heat and let cool completely.
2. Preheat oven to 375°.
3. In a medium bowl, beat cream cheese, lemon zest, 1 egg, and remaining 3 table-spoons granulated sugar with a mixer at medium speed until smooth; set aside.
4. On separate sheets of parchment paper, roll out each puff pastry sheet into a 12x10-inch rectangle. Spread cream cheese mixture down center third of each pastry, leaving a 3-inch border on long sides and a 1-inch bor-der on short sides. Using a sharp knife, cut 1-inch diagonal strips in pastries on either side of cream cheese mixture. Spoon cherry mixture over cream cheese mixture. Fold top and bottom of pastry over filling. Braid pastry strips over filling, tucking ends under pastry.
5. In a small bowl, lightly beat remaining egg. Brush pastries with egg wash, and sprinkle with turbinado sugar.
6. Transfer danishes with parchment to baking sheets. Bake until pastry is golden brown, 35 to 40 minutes. Serve warm or at room temperature.

Note: Cherry mixture may be made up to 3 days ahead.

SAVORING THE FEAST

Possibly no meal is more lovingly planned than our Christmas dinner. A ritual steeped in tradition, it offers a blissfully familiar array of dishes that have been passed from generation to generation. A menu often derived from family origins and time-honored customs, this most celebratory repast always comes together with the help of many hands, many hearts, and many well-kept secrets.

Clockwise from above left: Featuring red Anjou pear, pomegranate arils, and blood orange, this tantalizing salad sings with flavor and color. The dish is dressed with delicate pear vinaigrette infused with a heady mixture of chopped fresh herbs. Golden Yeast Rolls are seasoned with browned butter and rosemary. In keeping with the gem-inspired color scheme of this holiday meal, our showy Roasted Root Vegetables contains multihued fingerling potatoes, haricots verts, and orange baby carrots flavored with balsamic vinegar, ground mustard, and garlic.

Above: The crown jewel of the Christmas feast, our Roasted Turkey is seasoned with rosemary, thyme, sage, and citrus zests and is garnished with a brilliant mix of herbs, hypericum berries, and kumquats. Left: Butternut Squash and Fennel Mash presents a golden alternative to the more traditional creamed potatoes. Bacon, garlic, and thyme complement the flavors of winter squash and fennel simmered in a buttery broth.

Inspire sweet dreams for a long winter's nap with scrumptious White Chocolate Mousse Cake scented with orange, frosted with vanilla-orange buttercream, and garnished with decadent white chocolate curls, kumquats, and orange blossoms. This recipe will be requested for years to come—the crème de la crème for any soirée during the holiday season.

RECIPE INDEX

Seasonal Green Salad with Pear Vinaigrette p.149

Makes 6 to 8 servings

1 (6-ounce) bag **spring mix lettuces**
1 head **frisée**, washed and trimmed
1 red **Anjou pear**, cored and thinly sliced
¼ cup **pomegranate arils**
1 **blood orange**, peeled and cut into segments
⅓ cup **toasted pecans**
6 to 8 slices **pancetta**, cooked and crumbled
Pear Vinaigrette (recipe follows)

In a large bowl, combine lettuces, frisée, pear, pomegranate arils, orange segments, toasted pecans, and pancetta. Drizzle with Pear Vinaigrette just before serving.

Pear Vinaigrette

Makes approximately 1½ cups

½ cup **pear nectar**
⅓ cup **Anjou pear vinegar***
¼ cup **mayonnaise**
2 tablespoons **Dijon mustard**
2 teaspoons chopped fresh **chives**
2 teaspoons chopped fresh **rosemary**
1 teaspoon chopped fresh **thyme**
1 teaspoon chopped fresh **tarragon**
½ teaspoon coarse **salt**
¼ teaspoon ground **black pepper**
½ cup **olive oil**

In a small bowl, combine pear nectar, pear vinegar, mayonnaise, and mustard; whisk until smooth. Add chives, rosemary, thyme, tarragon, salt, and pepper; whisk to combine. Continue whisking, and slowly drizzle in olive oil. Store in an airtight container in the refrigerator for up to 2 weeks. Whisk before serving.

For testing purposes, our test kitchen used Cuisine Perel D'Anjou Pear Vinegar, which can be purchased at some supermarkets or online at cuisineperel.com.

Browned Butter–Rosemary Yeast Rolls p.149

Makes about 30

¼ cup warm **water** (105° to 115°)
2 (¼-ounce) packages **active dry yeast**
1½ cups warm **half-and-half** (105° to 115°)
½ cup **browned butter***, melted
5 tablespoons **sugar**
2½ teaspoons **salt**
3 large **eggs**, divided
3 cups **all-purpose flour**
3 cups **bread flour**
¼ cup **cultured buttermilk powder**†
3 tablespoons fresh **rosemary**

1. In a small bowl, combine water and yeast; let stand until foamy, about 5 minutes. In a large bowl, whisk together half-and-half, butter, sugar, salt, and 2 eggs. Add yeast mixture, whisking to combine.
2. In a separate large bowl, combine all-purpose flour, bread flour, cultured buttermilk powder, and rosemary. Add flour mixture to yeast mixture, 1 cup at a time, until a soft dough is formed. Turn dough out onto a floured work surface. Knead dough until elastic and smooth, about 8 to 10 minutes.
3. Spray the inside of a bowl with cooking spray; place dough in bowl, and turn to coat. Cover bowl with plastic film sprayed with cooking spray. Let stand in a warm, draft-free place (85°) until doubled in size, about 45 minutes.
4. Butter a 13x9x2-inch baking pan. On a lightly floured work surface, roll dough to a ¼-inch thickness. Using a 3-inch round cutter, cut as many rounds from dough as possible, rerolling scraps no more than once.
5. Shape dough rounds into small balls. Arrange dough balls in buttered pan. Cover pan with plastic wrap sprayed with cooking spray. Let stand in a warm, draft-free place (85°) until doubled in size, about 45 minutes.
6. Preheat oven to 350°.
7. In a small bowl, whisk remaining egg until smooth. Using a pastry brush, coat rolls evenly with egg. Bake until deep golden brown, 20 to 25 minutes. Remove from oven; let cool for 10 to 15 minutes. Serve immediately.

In a medium saucepan with a heavy bottom, melt butter over medium-high heat. Cook, watching closely, until butter foams and turns golden in color and has a nutty aroma, 8 to 10 minutes. Immediately remove from heat, and strain through a fine-mesh sieve. Let cool to room temperature.

†Cultured buttermilk powder is pasteurized and homogenized milk that has been inoculated with a culture of lactic-acid bacteria to simulate naturally occurring bacteria in the old-fashioned product.*

Roasted Root Vegetables with Haricots Verts p.149

Makes 6 to 8 servings

½ cup **balsamic vinegar**
¼ cup **olive oil**
2 tablespoons finely **ground mustard**
1 tablespoon **sour cream**
1 tablespoon chopped fresh **tarragon**
2½ teaspoons **coarse salt**
1 teaspoon ground **black pepper**
2 (12-ounce) packages **fingerling potatoes**
2 (8-ounce) packages **haricots verts**
1 (16-ounce) package **baby carrots**, tops attached
6 cloves **garlic**, peeled

1. Preheat oven to 400°. Line a rimmed baking sheet with aluminum foil.
2. In a small bowl, combine vinegar, olive oil, mustard, sour cream, tarragon, salt, and pepper; whisk until smooth.
3. In a large bowl, combine potatoes, haricots verts, carrots, and garlic. Pour vinegar mixture over vegetables, stirring to combine.
4. Place mixture on prepared baking sheet. Bake until tender, about 20 minutes. Serve immediately.

Citrus-and-Herb-Roasted Turkey p.150

Makes 8 servings

2 cups **butter**, softened
¼ cup chopped fresh **rosemary**
3 tablespoons chopped fresh **chives**
3 tablespoons minced **garlic**
2 tablespoons chopped fresh **thyme**
2 tablespoons **lemon zest**
2 tablespoons **coarse salt**
2 tablespoons ground **black pepper**
1 tablespoon **orange zest**
1 tablespoon **lime zest**
1 tablespoon chopped fresh **sage**
1 tablespoon **crushed red pepper**
1 (12- to 15-pound) **whole turkey**, washed, giblets and neck removed
Garnish: fresh **herbs**, **hypericum berries**, and **kumquats**

1. Preheat oven to 325°.

2. In a medium bowl, combine butter, rosemary, chives, garlic, thyme, lemon zest, salt, black pepper, orange zest, lime zest, sage, and crushed red pepper. Place turkey, breast side up, on a rack in a roasting pan; pat dry with paper towels.

3. Evenly rub butter mixture under and onto turkey skin and inside turkey cavity. Truss legs with butcher's twine. Cover with foil, and bake for 2 hours. Remove foil and continue to bake, basting occasionally with pan juices, until a meat thermometer inserted in thickest portion registers 165°, about 1½ hours more. Remove from oven, and let rest for 10 minutes. Garnish with herbs, hypericum berries, and kumquats, if desired.

Butternut Squash and Fennel Mash p.150
Makes 6 to 8 servings

8 slices **bacon**
3 tablespoons **butter**
1 clove **garlic**, minced
1 head **fennel**, trimmed and chopped
1 small **butternut squash** (about 2 pounds), peeled, seeded, and chopped
3 teaspoons **coarse salt**
2 teaspoons ground **black pepper**
½ cup **milk**
½ cup **heavy whipping cream**
Garnish: crumbled **bacon**, fresh **thyme leaves**

1. In a large Dutch oven, cook bacon over medium-high heat, turning frequently, until browned, 8 to 10 minutes. Remove bacon, reserving 3 tablespoons drippings. Let bacon cool completely; crumble.

2. Add butter to reserved bacon drippings. Add garlic and cook over medium-high heat for 2 to 3 minutes, stirring constantly. Add fennel, squash, salt, and pepper. Cover with 1 inch water. Bring to a boil; reduce heat and simmer over medium-high heat until tender, 15 to 20 minutes.

3. Drain in a large colander; return squash and fennel to pot. Stir over medium heat until dry, 2 to 3 minutes. Add milk and cream; mash with a potato masher until creamy or desired consistency is reached. Garnish with reserved bacon and thyme, if desired.

Orange-Scented White Chocolate Mousse Cake p.151
Makes 1 (3-layer) 9-inch cake

1 cup **unsalted butter**, softened
2 cups **granulated sugar**
2 teaspoons **vanilla extract**
1 teaspoon **orange extract**
1 teaspoon **orange zest**
3 cups **cake flour**
3 teaspoons **baking powder**
½ teaspoon **salt**
¼ teaspoon ground **cardamom**
¼ teaspoon ground **coriander**
1 cup **buttermilk**
5 **egg whites**, beaten until stiff
White Chocolate–Orange Mousse (recipe follows)
Vanilla-Orange Buttercream (recipe follows)
Garnish: **white-chocolate curls**, **kumquats**, and **orange blossoms**

1. Preheat oven to 350°. Spray 3 (9-inch) cake pans with baking spray; line with parchment rounds, and spray again.

2. In a large bowl, beat butter with a mixer at medium speed until creamy, about 4 minutes. Gradually add sugar, beating until fluffy, about 5 minutes. Beat in vanilla extract, orange extract, and orange zest.

3. In a small bowl, combine cake flour, baking powder, salt, cardamom, and coriander; sift twice. Add flour mixture to butter mixture alternately with buttermilk, beginning and ending with flour mixture. Gently fold in beaten egg whites.

4. Pour batter evenly into prepared pans. Bake until a wooden pick inserted near the centers comes out clean, 20 to 25 minutes. Let cool in pans for 10 minutes. Remove cakes from pans, and let cool completely on wire racks.

5. Spread half of White Chocolate–Orange Mousse between two cake layers; top with remaining mousse and remaining cake layer. Spread Vanilla-Orange Buttercream over top and sides of cake. Use any remaining buttercream to pipe around edges, if desired. Garnish with white chocolate curls, kumquats, and orange blossoms, if desired. Refrigerate for up to 5 days.

White Chocolate–Orange Mousse
Makes approximately 4 cups

1½ (4-ounce) bars **white chocolate**, chopped
1½ cups **heavy whipping cream**, divided
¼ cup **water**
2 tablespoons **orange liqueur**
1 (0.25-ounce) package (or 1 teaspoon) **unflavored gelatin**
1 teaspoon **orange zest**
¼ cup **confectioners' sugar**

1. In a medium bowl, combine white chocolate and ¼ cup cream. Microwave on high in 30-second intervals, stirring between each, until white chocolate is melted and smooth (about 1½ minutes total).

2. In a small saucepan, bring ¼ cup water and liqueur to a boil over high heat; remove from heat. Pour mixture into a small bowl. Sprinkle with gelatin; let sit until dissolved, about 5 minutes. Add gelatin mixture to white-chocolate mixture, stirring occasionally, until cooled, about 20 minutes.

3. In a medium bowl, beat orange zest, confectioners' sugar, and remaining 1¼ cups cream with a mixer at medium-high speed until soft peaks form.

4. Add one-third of whipped cream to chocolate mixture; beat at low speed until smooth. Add remaining cream mixture; beat at medium speed until stiff peaks form. Refrigerate 1 hour.

Vanilla-Orange Buttercream
Makes approximately 4 cups

3 **egg whites**
1 teaspoon **orange liqueur**
1 teaspoon **vanilla extract**
1 cup **granulated sugar**
1 cup **unsalted butter**, cut into tablespoons and softened
2 teaspoons **orange zest**

1. In the work bowl of a stand mixer set over a pan of simmering water, whisk egg whites, liqueur, vanilla extract, and sugar until mixture reaches 140° on a candy thermometer.

2. Place bowl on a stand mixer fitted with the whisk attachment; beat mixture at high speed until glossy and cool, about 10 minutes. Reduce mixer speed to medium-low. Add butter, 1 tablespoon at a time, until combined. Add orange zest. Replace whisk attachment with paddle attachment; beat until smooth.

THE CHRISTMAS TEA PARTY

TEXT ELAINE MELLEN

U npacking holiday adornments and readying my home for Yuletide, my heart fills with joy as I reminisce on celebrations of Christmases past. I linger in this quiet space, awaiting my grown children's return home while savoring the memory of a special teatime when my daughter, Mandi, now a new mother of a daughter, was just five years old. It was the first Christmas in our new house, and we decided to commemorate the move by inviting her girlfriends and their mothers to a tea party and cookie swap.

Mandi and I share many things, including our love of tea, baking, and Christmastime, so hosting this event was a delightful addition to our annual festivities. We decked our halls, baked copious assortments of cookies, purchased our favorite seasonal tea, and created a lovely invitation. For this inaugural occasion, we focused particular attention on décor, poring over magazines for ideas to replicate in our house. We spent hours trimming our interiors and finding appropriate accompaniments for the soirée. We washed vintage teacups passed down to us from Nana, polished the silver, and ironed linen napkins, along with a charming holiday tablecloth. Giving thought to every minute detail, we fashioned our own version of a magical tea party, complete with miniature teacup ornaments inscribed with guests' names and the date to offer as keepsakes.

The busy day before our fête was spent making homemade blueberry scones, clotted cream, and dainty tea sandwiches with a tantalizing selection of fillings: cream cheese–watercress spread, curried chicken salad, shrimp mousse, kalamata tapenade, and roast beef.

Preparations reached a fever pitch as the hour of the party neared, with my daughter and me putting the finishing touches on our dining room table—china glistening, candle flames reflecting off the silver, and fresh flowers brimming from a crystal vase. Potpourri simmering on the stove wafted a welcoming aroma throughout our abode. The final detail was to ready hot water for steeping the tea, along with arranging refreshments on designated serving platters. Equally excited, Mandi and I eagerly awaited the arrival of our guests.

Little girls dressed up in their Christmas finery, bringing their best manners, descended on our home to sip tea, taste delectable fare, and sing Christmas carols, all with girlish delight. In their holiday party dresses, the children were transformed, if only for a few hours, into graceful young ladies balancing plates and teacups without a spill while using please and thank you with ease.

At the close of the party, each mother-daughter pair received a holiday plate with a sampling of cookies brought for the exchange. I don't know, in retrospect, which generation was more delighted with the gathering. As the years passed, we mothers built lasting relationships through sharing significant milestones. Although our children are now busy with careers and raising their own families, we continue our tradition of coming together at Christmastime, along with our daughters, to celebrate enduring friendships. Each time we meet, the years just slip away, transporting us back to their childhoods for a festive Christmas tea party. For a few hours, I remember these women as they were so many Christmases ago—wee ones giddy with awe, dressed in party clothes, sipping tea, and eating delectable morsels—their innocent eyes glistening with holiday glee!

This year, the season is especially poignant, as we welcome Mandi's daughter, Madeline, to the celebration. Planning my infant granddaughter's first Christmas tea, my heart brews with love as I deck the halls, ready accoutrements, and plan the menu, all along savoring the cornucopia of memories from that initial occasion almost thirty years ago.

Before the flurry of activity associated with the bustling holiday season captures my days, I find repose with a cup of tea and reflect on how a seemingly insignificant decision, like choosing to host a Christmas tea for childhood companions, entwined our lives like a jewel-toned thread woven through a beautiful tapestry. We continue creating a legacy of memories, one sip at a time.

Giving from the
HEART

*The "hap-happiest season of all," as suggested in
"It's the Most Wonderful Time of the Year," allows for
the merriest of gatherings, where loved ones celebrate
'round a twinkling evergreen. Though the tradition
of exchanging pretty packages and thoughtful gifts
warms the soul, perhaps the true spirit of Christmas
cannot be wrapped in paper or tied with a shiny bow.*

TOKENS OF AFFECTION

Whether petite enough to tuck into a stocking or so large only a satin ribbon will do, thoughtfully given treasures create cherished memories.

'T is the season for giving—packages wrapped in colorful papers and tied with bows surround our Christmas trees, cookies baked with love are exchanged in tins and boxes, and pots of poinsettias and fragrant evergreens are delivered to the surprise and delight of the receivers. The kinship of the holidays brings out the best in all of us—we feel a touch more generous, a bit more openhearted. Christmas is the perfect occasion to show our friends and family how much they mean to us with little (or large) tokens of affection.

We all can recall the first time we found a present from Santa Claus. A baby doll in a lacy dress, a brand-new bicycle with tassels on the handle, or maybe a puppy with a floppy red bow around its neck magically appeared on Christmas morning beneath the tree. It was an enchanting feeling to know that the item had been chosen specifically for you. The same rings true for presents we exchange as adults—the thought and emotion behind them are far more important than the offerings themselves. More meaningful are the objects that hold sentimental value—those that have been selected expressly for us by the ones who know us best. Similarly, the act of giving can be a gift in and of itself. What a true delight to see the recipient's face light up with the recognition that this token was, in fact, bought or made with her personality and preferences in mind.

Giving the gift of our time is just as appreciated as a purchased present, especially during the holidays. Whether by volunteering at a soup kitchen or a women's shelter, or by spending the evening reconnecting with an old friend, the spirit of Christmas encourages us to share a part of ourselves with others.

The most wonderful time of the year calls for unwrapping holiday-themed pajamas to don on Christmas Eve and swapping decadent confections with friendly neighbors. Happy hearts anticipate these beloved gifting traditions, and in the spirit of generosity there is always an opportunity to invite new company to the exchange each year. The gift of togetherness marks each participant with Yuletide cheer.

THE WORLD

good
Tidings
to you

SEASON'S
Greetings

JUST
FOR
YOU

For those with a penchant for crafting, sparkling garland and gilded bells add a touch of whimsy to traditional gift wrap. For the tea lover, pretty paper doilies find new life when layered atop smaller boxes. Recipients of these thoughtful favors will certainly enjoy the contents within, as well as the fragrant cinnamon sticks attached to the charming bow.

YULETIDE MAGIC

Like a star atop the tree, unique embellishments adorning stacks of presents delight the eye and reflect a gift-giver's signature style.

E ven a small token can look magnificent when wrapped with care. A fashionable array of gift-wrapping paper is available, both on rolls and as flat sheets, and can be supplemented by art papers such as those used for scrapbooking. Satin, organza, or grosgrain ribbon tied in a gorgeous bow puts the finishing touch on the package. Items such as Christmas ornaments, faux holly berries, and even buttons add a little something extra when attached to a wrapped gift.

For friends who love to collect seasonal décor, a holiday ornament of faux mistletoe fastened to a parcel becomes a treasured keepsake. An outdoor stroll offers a plethora of trimmings. From iridescent feathers to a bundle of crimson roses, Mother Nature lends her winter finery to Father Christmas.

CYCLE OF LIFE

TEXT MILLY DAY

I t was a Christmas morning long ago. I had dreamed for weeks about the gifts I hoped to receive. Would it be that beautiful doll with the pink organdy dress, long ringlets, and eyes that opened and closed? Would it be a storybook about dogs? Surely, it would be a new nightgown and robe, and maybe, just maybe, that plaid taffeta dress that my mother and I had spied the week before in the department store window.

I awoke early—actually, I probably only slept for a few hours—convinced that the appointed hour of 6:00 a.m. would never arrive. And then I heard my father's voice: "Come on! Santa has been here, and you can come out."

I rushed up the stairs and entered the living room. It was still dark outside, and the lights of the tree caught my gaze. As I looked around the room, I saw it—there, to the side of the tree, tucked in the corner—a blue Schwinn bicycle. *Oh*, I thought, *how nice, a bike for my sister*. But then I saw another bicycle on the other side of the tree, back by the piano. A red one. *Oh, no, he couldn't have; he wouldn't have*. I didn't want this. How awful. I couldn't even ride a bike. Why would Santa get me a bike? My heart fell.

At breakfast, I was told that it was time to learn to ride a bicycle. So, after the dishes were cleared away, off we went, my father and me. First, I tried to mount the bike from the curb, and after a few attempts, I seemed to get the hang of it. Of course, all the while he was holding on to the back of the seat as I kept pleading, "Daddy, don't let go, don't let go."

His response was always, "Keep pedaling, honey, just keep pedaling."

He would run along beside me until I managed to do something to mess it up. I guess I just stopped pedaling. Then he would try again.

Oh, how I wished he would give up. But each day when he got home from work, I knew he would call me to get my bike and meet him in front of the house. And one afternoon, a miracle happened. Well, it was a miracle to me—and I'm sure to the neighbors who had begun to watch my riding lessons. I took off all on my own.

My dad had known the right moment to let go, and off I had pedaled down our street. "Keep pedaling!" he'd shouted when I started to falter. "Keep pedaling, honey."

Finally, Christmas vacation was over. I asked very courageously at dinner one night if I could ride my bike to school. I didn't expect him to let me, as we lived on a pretty steep hill and I would have to cross a busy boulevard. But to my surprise, he replied yes without any hesitation.

So the next morning, with my lunch pail in my basket, I started off. I rode for two or three blocks before I caught sight of our family car in the corner of my eye. *Oh, my, he's following me to school*. But he hung back a couple of blocks until I finally crossed that busy street, and then he honked and waved and went on to work.

It was after he left me that I experienced the real gift from my father: the thrill of independence, of being on my own, of feeling confident. I was free. No more rides to school. I could do it myself.

This incident lay on an old dusty shelf of my memory until many years later when our oldest daughter asked to ride her bike to school. Without much thought I said, "Of course." But then, as she started to get on her bike and pedal away, I got scared. What if she fell or encountered danger?

I raced into the garage, got into my car, and followed her all the way to school, just in case. As I was driving back home, I realized what great courage my dad had possessed when he allowed me to pedal off that morning so long ago. I wondered how he had known when to let go.

Seeing the LIGHTS

As thoughts turn to the holiday season, it is heartwarming to remember that Christmas is a universal celebration. While some children hang stockings at the mantel, others leave shoes outside their doors—all dreaming of wished-for goodies. The Yuletide spirit unites the world in a shimmering, glimmering time of shared jubilation.

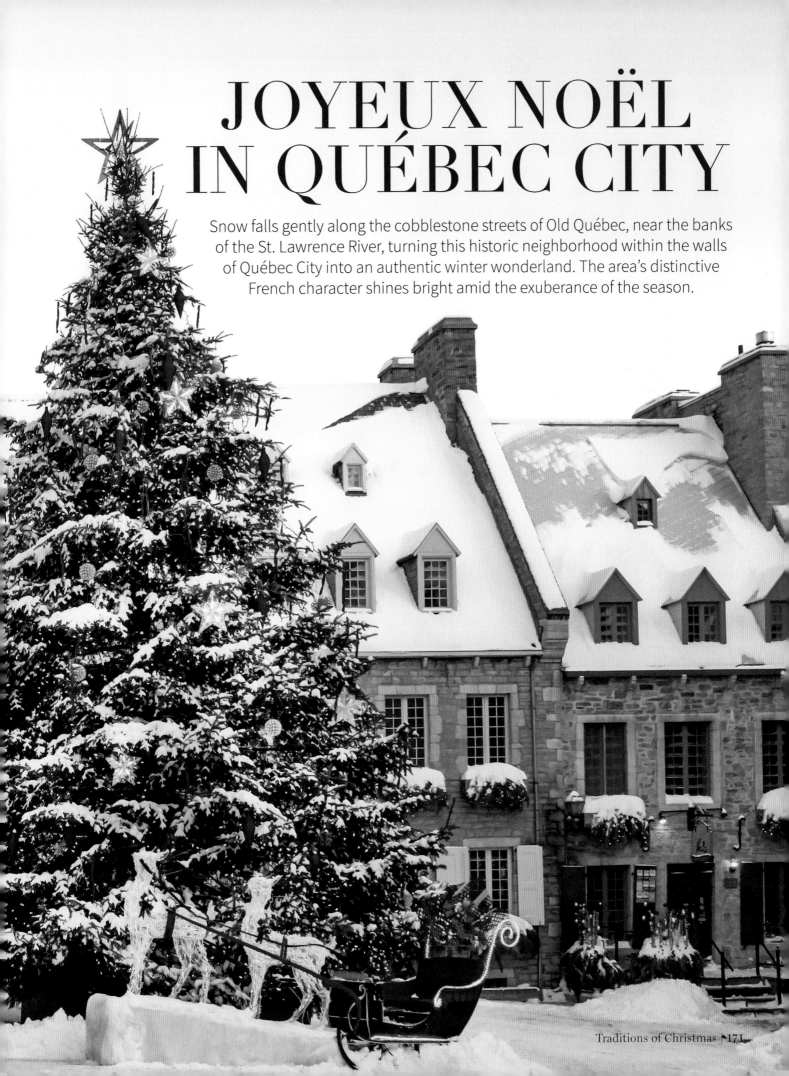

JOYEUX NOËL IN QUÉBEC CITY

Snow falls gently along the cobblestone streets of Old Québec, near the banks of the St. Lawrence River, turning this historic neighborhood within the walls of Québec City into an authentic winter wonderland. The area's distinctive French character shines bright amid the exuberance of the season.

LOWER TOWN

Famed French explorer and cartographer Samuel Champlain, called "The Father of New France," established the oldest section of Québec City in 1608. The area known as Lower Town brims with historic buildings, from churches and theaters to museums and performance venues, as well as the remains of Champlain's original settlement, which centers around the Place Royale. In December, when twinkling lights and tinsel-strung streets form a magical path to shops and restaurants, the riverside neighborhood of Petit-Champlain, shown opposite and this page, is the very vision of a Christmas card. Over the last decade or so, frescoes depicting the Old City's storied heritage have been revitalizing once plain buildings while treating passersby to scenes from the city's past.

UPPER TOWN

Opposite: Located on this site since 1647, the Notre-Dame de Québec Basilica-Cathedral was rebuilt twice after devastating fires, but even those unfortunate events could not diminish its spectacular beauty. The first church in the city to be built of stone, its façade was reconstructed in the 1840s to resemble that of Sainte-Geneviève in Paris. Famed French Canadian architect, painter, and sculptor François Baillairgé created the breathtaking baldachin, which dominates the domed ceiling. This ornate golden canopy appears to float above the altar, though in reality, it rests upon the chancel walls. This page: Built in 1870, the Terrasse Dufferin, above, overlooks the St. Lawrence River. With its advantageous riverfront location, Upper Town was the site of Fort Saint Louis, offering a military presence to the fledgling settlement. Battlefields Park, including the lovely Plains of Abraham, shown below left, now hosts Winter Carnival events. Though the area is still the center of city administration, a plethora of European-themed restaurants, bakeries, groceries, and shops has made it a mecca for epicureans.

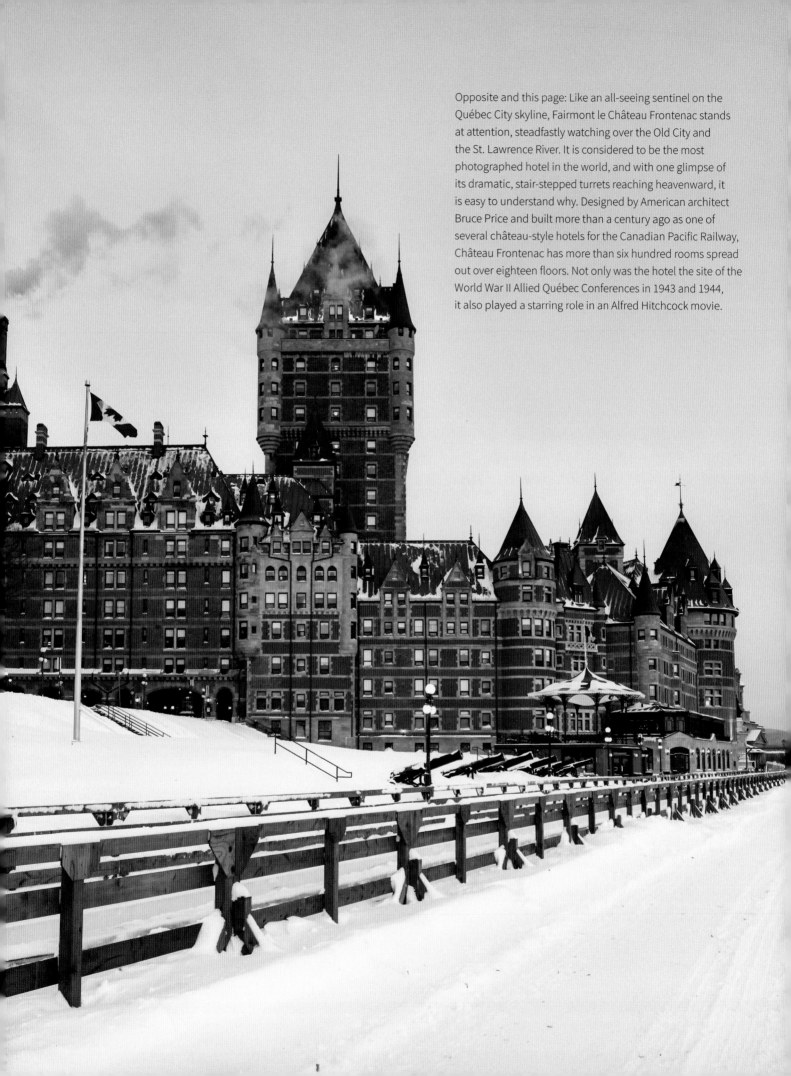

Opposite and this page: Like an all-seeing sentinel on the Québec City skyline, Fairmont le Château Frontenac stands at attention, steadfastly watching over the Old City and the St. Lawrence River. It is considered to be the most photographed hotel in the world, and with one glimpse of its dramatic, stair-stepped turrets reaching heavenward, it is easy to understand why. Designed by American architect Bruce Price and built more than a century ago as one of several château-style hotels for the Canadian Pacific Railway, Château Frontenac has more than six hundred rooms spread out over eighteen floors. Not only was the hotel the site of the World War II Allied Québec Conferences in 1943 and 1944, it also played a starring role in an Alfred Hitchcock movie.

Originally designed to be the ultimate stopover for railway travelers, Château Frontenac has hosted such notables as Queen Elizabeth II, Princess Grace of Monaco, and Charles Lindbergh in its century-plus past. It continues to play a part in providing memorable experiences for visitors to the area, with luxurious accommodations that embody all the elegance of the grand European hotels, including the private-concierge Fairmont Gold floors. Each of Château Frontenac's dining options offers breathtaking views of the St. Lawrence River, from afternoon tea—complete with scones and Devonshire cream—to five-course dinners inspired by the flavors of the season.

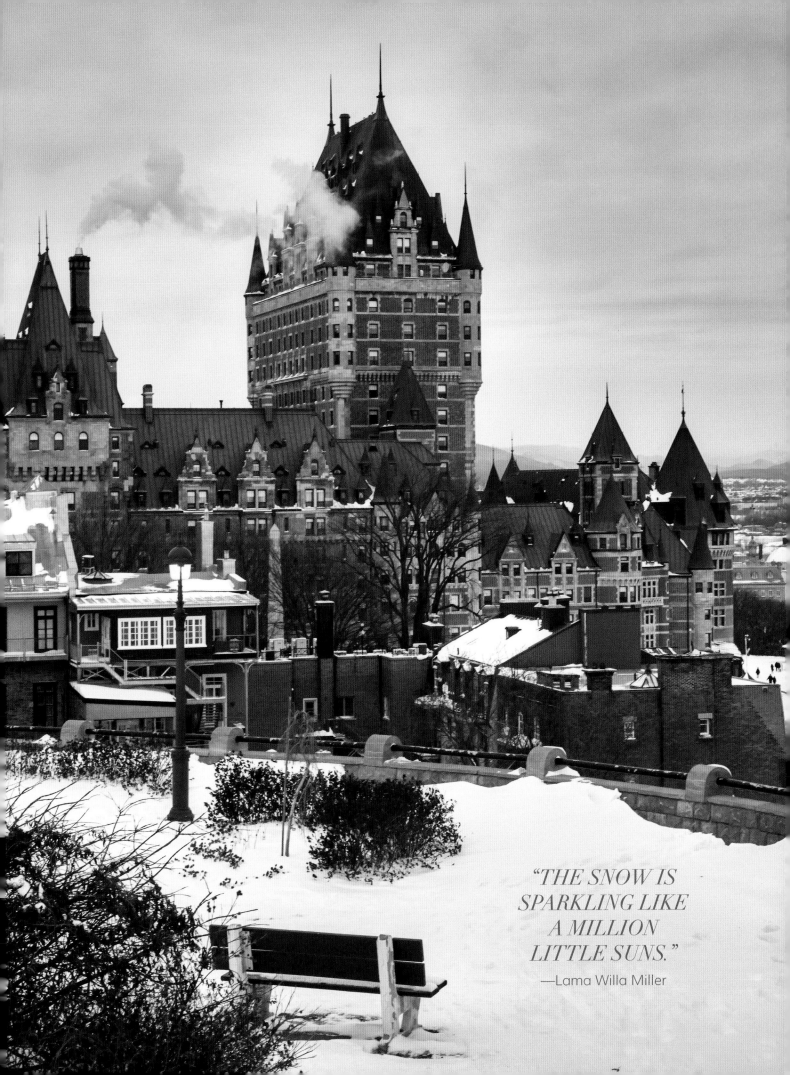

"THE SNOW IS
SPARKLING LIKE
A MILLION
LITTLE SUNS."
—Lama Willa Miller

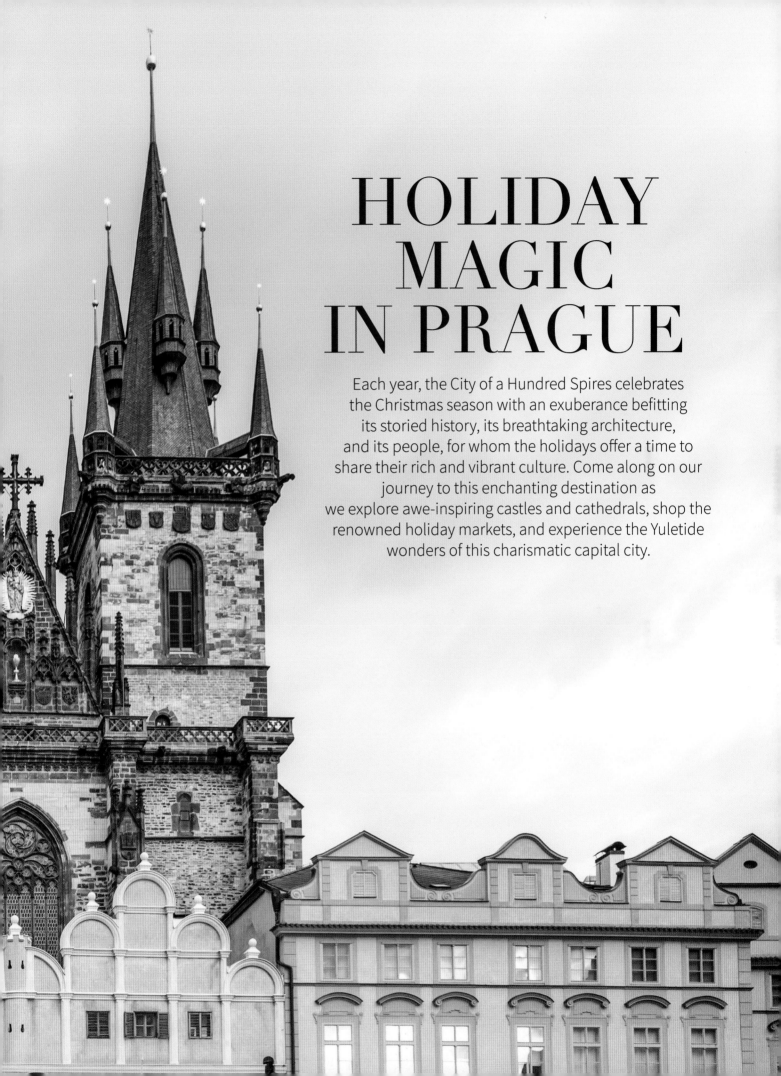

HOLIDAY MAGIC IN PRAGUE

Each year, the City of a Hundred Spires celebrates the Christmas season with an exuberance befitting its storied history, its breathtaking architecture, and its people, for whom the holidays offer a time to share their rich and vibrant culture. Come along on our journey to this enchanting destination as we explore awe-inspiring castles and cathedrals, shop the renowned holiday markets, and experience the Yuletide wonders of this charismatic capital city.

Above: Architect Hans Vlach designed the Renaissance-style Rosenberg Palace for the eponymous family. Later, it served as a residence for unmarried ladies of patrician rank. Opposite: St. Vitus Cathedral, the largest church in Prague, was the customary coronation site of Czech kings and queens, as well as the final resting place for several sovereigns, patron saints, archbishops, and aristocrats.

Nestled in the heart of Europe, the Czech Republic—also called Czechia—is a country blessed with beauty and an interesting narrative that dates to fourth century B.C., when it was settled by the Celtic Boii tribe and originally christened "Bohemia." As its capital, Prague has been at the center of Czech life for centuries, and the city enjoys a sterling reputation for its dedication to the arts and its stunning architecture, which encompasses a variety of styles, from Romanesque and Gothic to Baroque and Moorish Revival. While a visit here is enjoyable in any season, at Christmastime, Prague is positively mesmeric as it hums with the holiday spirit.

Sheltered beneath the twin Gothic towers of the Church of Our Lady before Týn, Old Town Square is the ever-bustling center of Yuletide festivities. A soaring evergreen, laden with baubles, tinsel, and glittering lights, is a bright beacon calling all to come to the famous Christmas markets clustered around the square. With the enticing aroma of spiced mulled wine and hot chocolate swirling in the chilled air, shoppers drift from stall to stall, sampling *párek* sausages and scrumptious *trdelnik* pastries, while perusing the marvelous array of wares.

Beyond the markets, there are many historical treasures that underscore the city's significant past. Resting atop a hill overlooking the town, Prague Castle was once the seat of power for the Bohemian kings, while the nearby Rosenberg Palace, built for that aristocratic family in the 1500s, later served as a home for unmarried women of nobility. The ancient Charles Bridge, spanning the scenic Vltava River, connects the castle grounds to Old Town, and the eighteenth-century Klementinum Library brims with both books and beautiful ceiling frescoes.

From festive markets filled with friendly vendors to hallowed edifices polished by time, a sojourn to Prague promises joyful surroundings for memorable holiday adventures.

Opposite: These whimsical glass ornaments are typical of the seasonal items on offer at Prague's markets, whether shoppers are looking for gifts for others or a trinket or two for themselves. This page, above: The medieval-era Charles Bridge was once the only pathway over the Vltava River. Commissioned by Charles IV, king of Bohemia and Holy Roman Emperor, the stone-arch bridge dates to 1357. Below right: Colored-glass vessels sparkle in a shop window.

Clockwise from above left: Stalls at the Old Town Square market brim with an array of wares, from sparkling Christmas baubles to cozy winter clothing. A breathtaking example of Baroque-period architecture, the magnificent St. Nicholas Church in Old Town dates to the 1730s. It hosts both religious services and, thanks to its perfect acoustics, classical music concerts. The towering spires of the Church of Our Lady before Týn rise above the square, while an ornate carving rests over the doorway of Klementinum Library and a touch of seasonal color stands out near the Strahov Monastery. Yuletide creativity abounds in the capital city, where elaborate wreaths are a common sight on both commercial and residential doors throughout Prague.

Traditions of Christmas | 187

VIENNESE WALTZ

Swags of twinkling lights crisscross the streets of historic Vienna, Austria, giving the illustrious area the look of a dazzling outdoor ballroom and lending a festive air to the city's magnificent holiday markets.

Above: The nineteenth-century Kunsthistorisches Museum Wien, evincing quintessential Renaissance Revival style, is one of Vienna's most acclaimed buildings, not only for its spectacular architecture but also for its ornate stucco-and-gold-leaf interiors.

Opposite, clockwise from below: Window-shoppers quickly become paying customers, thanks to the stores' enticing displays. The grounds of this iconic building are the site of the MuseumsQuartier market. This page, clockwise from above left: The bright and colorful tile roof of St. Stephen's Cathedral makes it an instantly recognizable landmark. A wondrous array of wares in each market stall makes easy work of Christmas shopping. In the center of the city, the Stephansplatz square sparkles throughout the holiday season with a sprawling canopy of glittering lights

Among the capital's many attractions are awe-inspiring houses of worship, including St. Peter's Church, above left, with an architectural design inspired by St. Peter's Basilica at the Vatican in Rome. The Viennese version dates to the early eighteenth century and features an iconic copper dome, which has acquired a beautiful verdigris patina through the years, making it one of the city's most picturesque buildings. Another notable sanctuary is St. Charles Church, center right, which was the last project of the illustrious Baroque architect Johann Bernhard Fischer von Erlach. The cupola features a series of ornate frescoes painted by von Erlach's lifelong friend and collaborator, Austrian-born artist Johann Michael Rottmayr.

The enticing aromas of roasted chestnuts and mulled wine mingle with the sounds of familiar carols and crowd chatter amid one of winter's most enduring traditions: Vienna's Christmas markets. More than twenty different emporia fan out from the heart of this history-rich place, each one brimming with assorted wares that run the gamut from gingerbread and candles to jewelry, clothing, and so much more.

The dozens of shops standing in the shadow of Schönbrunn Palace are particularly stellar. The summer residence of Habsburg royalty in centuries past, the rococo-style castle traces its beginnings to 1642 and forms a majestic backdrop to the handcrafted Nativity scenes, decorations, and other items offered here. Situated halfway between Schönbrunn and the legendary Danube River, The Hofburg served as the Habsburgs' winter quarters. The markets located in this sprawling complex rub shoulders with Roman ruins, the ancient St. Michael's Church, and a former home of Austrian composer Joseph Haydn.

Vienna offers much to experience beyond the shopping venues. Since it first opened in 1869, the Vienna State Opera has welcomed the works of Mozart to Mahler. Though damaged by bombs during World War II, the venue quickly rebounded and is considered one of the world's best opera houses. Historic churches, such as St. Charles Church and St. Stephen's Cathedral, are ecclesiastical wonders.

Home to the renowned torte that bears its name, Hotel Sacher has earned its five-star ranking with personal service and superlative accommodations. In a town known for its coffeehouses, there are plenty of options for enjoying a cup of Vienna's signature mélange brew, accompanied by sweet apple strudel. After all, it takes plenty of sustenance to cover the breadth of this enchanted city's vibrant array of seasonal attractions.

Hotel Sacher draws patrons to its luxurious quarters with sumptuous bedding, fine dining, private terraces, and a spa featuring unique, chocolate-based treatments, but it might be the establishment's signature Sacher-Torte that proffers the sweetest dreams. A fixture since 1876, the hostelry has welcomed many notable guests, from renowned ballet dancer Rudolf Nureyev to Queen Elizabeth II.

MOZART

Opposite: Since its opening production of Mozart's much celebrated work *Don Giovanni* in 1869, the Vienna State Opera House has enjoyed a well-earned reputation for artistic excellence. The interiors are simply breathtaking, with stunning frescoes, busts of notable composers, and plenty of gilded decoration. This page, above left: The ancient St. Michael's Church, the oldest parts of which date to the thirteenth century, lies across the square from The Hofburg. It is one of very few Romanesque buildings left in Vienna, though later additions have introduced other architectural styles, from Gothic to Baroque.

Schönbrunn Palace may have been the summertime getaway for the Habsburg royals, but during the winter holidays, it is a mecca for shoppers who thrill to the wares offered at the market assembled on its forecourt. With the regal residence presenting an elegant backdrop, it's no wonder the offerings are equally refined—with an emphasis on exquisite arts and crafts—while brass band and choir concerts add to the festive ambiance.

PALEIS HET LOO: A CASTLE AT YULETIDE

The swirling maze of parterres in the palace gardens is crowned with an icy layer of snow—a crystalline welcome for visitors to this centuries-old royal residence in the Netherlands.

Above: Even the front gates are trimmed in gold at Paleis Het Loo— just a hint of the opulence that lies within this centuries-old estate. Every November finds this entrance open in welcome to the thousands of visitors arriving to attend the Spirit of Winter festival, with its myriad activities and markets brimming with wares.

More than three hundred years ago, Prince William III of Orange, the newly appointed Stadtholder of Gelderland in the Netherlands, was drawn to the heather-covered hills that promised plenty of sport for the avid hunter and his frequent guests. Although a nearby house was renovated to serve as a hunting lodge, he soon purchased a property where the old castle of Het Loo (Dutch for "clearing in the woods") stood outside the town of Apeldoorn. In keeping with the prince's royal status, a new and grander residence was erected on the grounds and christened Paleis Het Loo.

As was customary at the time, the Dutch-Baroque structure was built symmetrically around a central axis, with mirror-image wings on either side. Rather than using the usual long corridors to connect various sections, the palace was divided into apartments, each one leading to the next.

Because the estate grounds were extraordinarily picturesque, great effort was made to blur the lines between indoor and outdoor spaces. The walls of the main hall and staircase were painted with fresco murals, and openwork gilded-iron gates led outside to the botanical splendor beyond. An attraction in and of themselves, the formal seventeenth-century gardens featured fountains and statues of Greek gods and goddesses interspersed among a series of parterres.

Although subsequent generations of sovereigns made numerous changes, a renovation begun in the 1970s restored the exterior to its former glory. A decade later, the mansion was converted into a museum so visitors could see its breathtaking opulence for themselves. Heraldic tapestries and rare paintings are displayed throughout the rooms, and gold fittings and fabrics gleam from ceiling to floor, as if King Midas had strolled the halls, touching everything in sight. The castle contains an immense assemblage of art, furniture, textiles, books, and more, with additional items on loan from national and private sources.

Each November, the gates of Paleis Het Loo open for the celebrated Spirit of Winter festival, where more than one hundred exhibitors and vendors offer an assortment of wares. Fairgoers can sample local gourmet dishes, watch demonstrations, and shop for gifts. In the shadow of this grand edifice, where countless monarchs celebrated centuries ago, the holiday season gets off to a perfectly regal start.

Below right: With its brilliant red walls and shimmering chandeliers, the drawing room of Stadtholder William V is the perfect milieu for a holiday dinner by candlelight. After undergoing an extensive renovation, the house was opened to the public in 1984, offering visitors a glimpse into the luxurious lifestyle of three centuries of royal residents. This lavishly appointed room features just a sampling of Het Loo's vast and enviable art collection. When the palace hosts the annual winter festival, shoppers find all sorts of seasonal goods, including traditional Dutch confections, such as *kerstkransjes* (wreath-shaped cookies), *boterkoek* (almond-butter cake), or Saint Nicholas pudding.

The Spirit of Winter festival celebrates the season with a variety of activities, from ice-skating and shopping to fashion shows and gourmet tastings. Vendors offer a plethora of goods in tentlike stalls arranged in neat rows across the grounds. Opposite, below right: Bilderberg Hotel De Keizerskroon was once owned by the Netherlands' beloved Queen Wilhemina. It retains its royal ambiance and offers close-by accommodations for festivalgoers. This page: Patrons are enchanted by imaginatively decorated stalls, above right, and unique displays, such as this lighted ball gown, above left.

A MERRY EXCURSION

Two hours south of Apeldoorn, the hamlet of Valkenburg aan de Geul truly embraces the Yuletide season. Colorfully decorated trees line the streets and the banks of the Geul river, bringing smiles to everyone's faces and a joyful Christmas cadence to pedestrians' steps as they check items off their shopping lists. The windows of downtown shops are filled with all manner of enticing wares—from fresh-cut greenery and floral arrangements to homemade breads and Limburg pies. Patrons are apt to discover delicate glass ornaments alongside antiques and home accessories. Twice each week during the holidays, townspeople and visitors alike turn out for festive parades, complete with floats and lively dancers. But some of Valkenburg's most popular attractions lie below ground, in the area's renowned caves, where bustling Christmas markets welcome shoppers all season long.

Savoring QUIETUDE

Amid the bustle and laughter of Yuletide, time imbued with stillness and contemplation answers the spirit's yearning for moments of gentle repose. These serene hours of musing, dreaming, and resting set the heart aglow with restored feelings of gratitude for the offerings of the merriest season.

THOUGHTFUL REFLECTIONS

Amid the busyness of the Christmas season, the tradition of Advent beckons one to spend time in quiet contemplation of the wonder of the season, whether observed during travels or from home.

For many congregants, houses of worship offer a cherished opportunity to focus on the spiritual meaning of Christmas. When the desire to attend sacred services mingles with a sense of wanderlust, New Orleans awaits with beautiful churches and cathedrals. Perhaps the most iconic is St. Louis Cathedral, shown above left and opposite, which stands sentinel at one end of Jackson Square.

PAISSEZ MES AGNEAUX

PAISSEZ MES BREBIS

There's no better time to visit the Crescent City than when it is decked to perfection for the holidays. Built in 1840 as the first Catholic church erected outside the French Quarter, St. Patrick's Church is located in the Central Business District. The sanctum features inspiring murals by artist Leon Pomarede.

Above: At the Immaculate Conception Jesuit Church, Archangel Michael and seven guardian angels are carved into interior columns, while cast-iron pews incorporate both emblems relating to the Virgin Mary and New Orleans' signature fleur-de-lis. Opposite: The nineteenth-century Christ Church Cathedral has evolved over time with the addition of Victorian stained-glass windows.

SOUNDS OF THE SEASON

TEXT CAROL BULLMAN

Each October, I begin to listen once again to the music that opens my heart. My husband smiles. My sisters and my mother, if they happen to visit while a carol is playing, roll their eyes and exclaim, "Too soon!" My children understand. They let the music carry their imaginations into the snow-sparkling month of December.

With each note, memories swell, one growing into another—like branches of a noble fir. The bottom ones are densest, for the early years of Christmas are thick with excitement and mystery.

Bing Crosby sings, and I am transported to my fifth Christmas, the year I heard the drumming of reindeer hooves atop our house. Later, I learned it was only pecan percussion, the nuts gathered and tossed onto the roof by my parents. Somehow, this seems no less magical to me: the shivering pair—my father humming a festive tune, my mother brimming with contentment—creating joy beneath a winter sky winking with stars.

Baking is never more pleasurable than when I'm enveloped in the gentle world Christmas carols evoke. I mix ingredients, and the remembrances start to flow of that glorious holiday when my father, his parents, and his four siblings gathered in front of the decorated tables full of children, spouses, and remnants of the feast. All at once, guided by my grandfather's operatic bass, they blended their voices—voices sewn from the same cloth, practiced and perfected, filling my heart like a prayer.

As a piano arrangement of "Silent Night" plays in my kitchen, I can almost hear my little sister's voice cracking. Amy had a cold the year Daddy decided to record each of his children singing. Wasn't that the same year he took us caroling in the dark—my sister Julie lugging her drum set? Baby Allison, who grew up to have perfect pitch, was too young to accompany us, but I pretended that we sounded like my father and his brother and sisters.

The boughs of Christmas memories grow sparser as I age, climbing ever closer to that radiant star. Still, the uppermost branches are the strongest of all, able to bear the weight of the heaviest adornment. These branches contain the sap of all Christmases past.

Now, my Yuletides are full of decorating, baking, organizing, shopping, and wrapping, but sparse in new, indelible moments. Every December awakens me with its life-giving touch, and a memory grows. Last year, a sturdy branch was strengthened when I unwrapped a gift from my father. From his old reel-to-reel recordings, he had burned a CD of his family singing seasonal standards. We inserted it, and the room, bustling with loved ones and crinkling wrapping paper, hushed to bear witness to our shared history.

My grandmother's soprano, as bright as snow-reflected sunshine, rings out "Sleigh Ride." My grandfather is alive again, his voice as solid as the sleigh. I imagine them with their five children, huddled warm against the cold, led by horses through winter vistas. Aunt Bonnie's pure 8-year-old voice begins "The Bells of Christmas Are Ringing." Uncle David and Aunt Becky join her—vocal bells chiming hope. Aunt Debbie harmonizes with my father as his 17-year-old hands coax clear notes from the same guitar he will one day play for his daughters and grandchildren. The music lifts my thoughts and brings me back to what is most important.

Whenever I listen to Christmas songs, I relive this memory and all those ringed within it and stacked deep beneath. Alone in my kitchen, no matter the month, I gather with my family 'round the tree.

COZY MOMENTS

Balancing the bustling pace of Yuletide is the call to slow down, to take a breath, and to savor precious hours of repose. Setting aside time for solitude becomes even more precious during this festive season.

Sitting down to pen greeting cards, organize the holiday calendar, or plan menus for seasonal entertaining is a peaceful pursuit when one's desk is set within the glow of a glittering Christmas tree.

Below and opposite: Holiday stresses melt away within the haven of a private sanctuary. The hurried pace of the season seems to ease as water flows into an Empire tub. Indulgent bath products, flickering candles, and silky pajamas pamper body and soul.

No matter the allure of distant places, nothing can compare to the supreme comfort of coming home to one's own abode. With the gentle aroma of evergreens extending a seasonal welcome and interiors arrayed in holiday adornments, this is sure to be a merry Christmas.

All that is left to do on this leisurely afternoon, as the sun is soon to fade, is to light candles and brew a pot of tea. Extra cups and saucers await in case a neighbor comes to call. Sipped in solitude or shared with a friend, the steaming blend promises moments of bliss.

THE FIRST SNOW

TEXT DEBORAH A. BENNETT

When I was a little girl, years ago, the first snowfall always came softly and silently as we walked home from school, down the long ribbon of street. So close to Christmas, we could feel the holiday tiptoeing up behind us, like the wind whistling through bare elm trees.

I remember gray tabby cats sitting on the garden walls and blackbirds with sparkling wings soaring by them while we lifted our chins to the sky—our mittened hands and the pom-pommed ends of our knitted hats flying as we skipped along the sidewalk. We laughed in delight as the snowflakes floated down and landed on our heads, the tips of our noses, and our eyelashes. Candles on the windowsills of nearby houses flickered like little moons, and strings of colored lights encircled the doors like stars glowing in the deepening sky.

Stashed inside our book bags and tucked into our coat pockets were carefully guarded felt angels, red-and-green paper chains, and pipe-cleaner snowflakes to adorn trees and garlanded mantels at home. In the lengthening shadows, with the last glint of winter light shining from behind an orange-and-silver bank of clouds, we sang songs about snowmen, sidewalk Santas ringing silver bells, and sleds sliding across frozen lakes and wide, sugary hills.

There, in the pale air hung with whispers—the whole world white and gray and still—we were as dazzled by our own wishes as by any tinsel or glistening icicles. Great gold-ribboned boxes, silver packages, and luminous red bags full of everything we ever wished for right out loud captivated us. We envisioned dollhouses big enough to sit in, tea sets with tiny blue flowers, cowboy boots, and bicycles with banana seats.

Then there were the secret wishes, the ones we made silently. For doors wide with hugs and kisses and voices full of laughter. For wild and noisy nights with sisters and brothers, cousins, and aunts and uncles—their songs and stories echoing in the enveloping warmth of the fire burning in the hearth, the tantalizing aroma of dinner wafting through the house, and the big day only one more sleep away.

I remember walking through the thickening, swirling flurry of snow and watching the breath escape from our mouths like smoke from little chimneys. We held hands as we crossed the street and then headed toward the sweet surprise of our own homes, stairs, and doorways. It felt more like Christmas with every step, like church bells had rung somewhere. In our hearts. In the air. Everywhere.

CREDITS & RESOURCES

Traditions of Christmas

Editor-in-Chief: Phyllis Hoffman DePiano

Editor: Melissa Lester

Senior Director of Design: Melissa Sturdivant Smith

Senior Writer: Karen Callaway

Associate Editor: Leslie Bennett Smith

Assistant Editor: Kassidy Abernathy

Administrative Senior Art Director: Tracy Wood-Franklin

Editorial Assistant: Lydia McMullen

Creative Director/Photography: Mac Jamieson

Senior Copy Editor: Meg Lundberg

Copy Editor: Michele Moore

Senior Digital Imaging Specialist: Delisa McDaniel

CONTRIBUTING WRITERS

DEBORAH A. BENNETT: page 224

CAROL BULLMAN: page 214

MILLY DAY: page 166

MARGARET HENDLEY: page 42

ELAINE MELLEN: page 154

CONTRIBUTING PHOTOGRAPHERS

JEAN ALLSOPP: pages 24–27

KIMBERLY FINKEL DAVIS: cover and pages 56–59

WILL DICKEY: page 30

ANNEKE GAMBON: pages 168 and 196–203

LAUREY GLENN: pages 14 and 30

KATE HEADLEY: pages 20–21 and 30

JANE HOPE: pages 180–195

MAC JAMIESON: pages 10, 12, 14, 16–18, 44–45, 114–117, 206–213, and 215

YUNHEE KIM: pages 170–179

JOHN O'HAGAN: pages 8, 36, 48–49, 92–101, 167, 220–221, and back cover

MARCY BLACK SIMPSON: pages 1, 4–6, 15, 19, 22, 30, 32, 34, 40–41, 46–47, 50–54, 84–91, 126–129, 146–150, 155–156, 158, 160–162, 165, 167, and 216–219

STEPHANIE WELBOURNE STEELE: pages 2, 13, 23, 30–31, 35–39, 43, 60–83, 102, 104–113, 118–124, 130–136, 140–142, 159, 163–164, 204, and 222–223

KAMIN WILLIAMS: pages 28–29

CONTRIBUTING STYLISTS

ANNE-EMORY BANKSTON: page 19

SIDNEY BRAGIEL: pages 14, 24–27, 30, 35–36, 48–49, and back cover

MARY JANE CALANDRA: page 164

JENNIFER CHAPMAN: pages 1, 4–5, 32, and 40–41

MISSIE NEVILLE CRAWFORD: page 35

KATHY ELLIS: pages 60–67 and 92–101

BRITTANY WILLIAMS FLOWERS: pages 20–21 and 30

MARY LEIGH GWALTNEY: cover and pages 28–31, 56–59, 156, 158, 160–162, and 165

YUKIE MCLEAN: pages 6, 50–54, 84–91, 126–129, 146–150, 216–217, and 222–223

MELISSA STURDIVANT SMITH: pages 8, 15, 23, 34, 36–39, 43, 46–47, 68–83, 102, 104–124, 130–136, 140–142, 159, 204, and 215

DONNA TRONOLONE: page 164

KATHLEEN COOK VARNER: pages 44–45

BETH K. WEIMER: page 155

CONTRIBUTING RECIPE DEVELOPERS AND FOOD STYLISTS:

JADE SINACORI: pages 130–139

REBECCA TREADWELL: pages 140–145

LOREN WOOD: pages 146–153 and 155

WHERE TO SHOP & BUY

Below is a listing of products and companies featured in this book.

Pages 1, 4–5, 15, 32, 34, and 40–41: Jennifer Chapman Design, 760-613-4613, jenniferchapmandesign.com.

Pages 2, 68–83 and 163: The Brittany House at Oak Hill, 5931 AL-21, Oak Hill, AL, 256-975-7616, thebrittanyhouseantiquesatoakhill.com.

Pages 10, 12, 14, and 16–18: Preservation Resource Center of New Orleans Holiday Tour, The Leeds-Davis Building, 923 Tchoupitoulas Street, New Orleans, LA, 504-581-7032, prcno.org.

Page 13: Designed by Moyanne Harding, I.D.S., 434-851-9421, moyanne.com.

Pages 14 and 30: Key Circle Press, 3241 Dell Road, Mountain Brook, AL, 205-936-5138, keycirclepress.com.

Pages 20–21: Special thanks to Leaf & Petal, 2817 Cahaba Road, Mountain Brook, AL, 205-871-3832, leafnpetal.com, and Sweet Peas Garden Shop, 2829 Linden Avenue, Homewood, AL, 205-879-3839, sweetpeasgardenshop.com.

Page 30: Special thanks to Laurel Limbaugh Patrick, laurellimbaugh.com, and Beth Singletary, bethsingletary.com. The Magnolia Company Fresh Bunches wreath, Fresh Bunches garland; 800-880-4662, themagnoliacompany.com.

Page 31: Argent Antiques, sterling silver salt and pepper shakers; 205-871-4221. Lenox: Floral Majesty dinner plate, Floral Majesty salad plate, Floral Majesty bread-and-butter plate, Floral Majesty teacup and saucer; Moser: Splendid goblet; Pickard China: Eisenhower charger; Saint Louis: Thistle goblet in gold; from Bromberg's, 205-871-3276, brombergs.com.

Page 35: Spencer Hatcher, artist, 251-656-5395.

Pages 36 and 48–49: Special thanks to homeowners Kimberly and Robert Post. Interiors by Kathy Harris, 3157 Cahaba Heights Road, Vestavia Hills, AL, 205-970-4161, interiorskh@att.net.

Pages 36 and 37: Caspari: Coromandel Gift Wrap Roll in Red High-Gloss Paper, Gilded Holly Gift Wrap Roll in Gold Foil Paper, Greek Meander Gift Wrap Roll in Green & Gold Foil Paper, Royal Plaid Gift Wrap Roll on Foil Paper; 434-817-7880, casparionline.com. D. Stevens Fine Ribbons: 4" Taffeta Plaid Ribbon; 623-582-9915, dstevensllc.com. Fig & Dove: Soft Gold Christmas Stocking, Cream Nobilis Christmas Stocking with Embroidered Cuff; info@figanddove.com, figanddove.com. Shishi: Various Ornaments; shishi.ee.

Page 38–39: Reliant Ribbon: gold ribbon; 844-444-1963, reliantribbon.com.

Page 43: Paper Source: Watercolor Garden Wrapping Paper, Gold Pine Branches Handmade Paper, Glittered Floral Velvet on Pink Handmade Paper, Gold Laurel Leaf on Cream Handmade Paper; 888-727-3711, papersource.com. Park Hill Collection: Wilderness Glass Cone Ornaments, Native Cedar Garland; 888-603-3334, shop.parkhillcollection.com. Samuel & Sons: Chevallerie Botanical Border in Macaron, Elise Embroidered Border in Alabaster, Mireille Embroidered Border in Petal; 212-704-8000, samuelandsons.com.

Pages 44–45: Special thanks to homeowners Lisa and Scott Maclellan.

Pages 46–47: Herend: Golden Laurel Service Plate, Golden Laurel Dinner Plate; 800-643-7363, herendusa.com. Kim Seybert: Frost Placemat in blush, Herringbone Napkin in white, gold, and silver; 877-564-7850, kimseybert.com. Moser: Royal Champagne glass, Royal White Wine glass; +420 730 550 520, moser.com. Oneida: Golden Michelangelo 5-Piece Place setting; 888-263-7195, oneida.com. Sasha Nicholas: Custom "V" with Crown Salad Plate; 888-877-5230, sashanicholas.com. Special thanks to Kim Cobb of Flying Squirrel Cookies, flyingsquirrelcookies@gmail.com; PRE Event Resources for providing gold chivari chairs and silk linens, 1209 James Harrison Jr. Parkway, Tuscaloosa, AL, 205-469-0105; Reliant Ribbon for providing all ribbons in blush, gold, and cream, 844-444-1963, reliantribbon.com; The University Club, 421 Queen City Avenue, Tuscaloosa, AL, 205-348-4848; Empress Stationery, empressstationery.com.

Pages 50–52: Dorothy McDaniel's Flower Market, 205-871-0092, dorothymcdaniel.com. Mary Charles Doll House: vintage dolls; 205-870-5544, mcdollhouse.com. Priester's Pecans: Pecan garland; 800-277-3226, priesters.com.

Pages 60–67 and 92–101: For more information about designer Kathy Ellis's work, contact her at kcthompto15@gmail.com or follow her @kathyellisfrenchkat on Instagram.

Pages 92–101: Special thanks to homeowners Cindy and Tim Morrison.

Pages 104–113: Special thanks to interior designer Jan Cash.

Pages 114–117: Bernardaud: Grenadiers Service Plate (Charger), Grenadiers Salad Plate, Grenadiers Flat Cup and Saucer Set; from Replacements, Ltd., 800-737-5223, replacements.com. Special thanks to Keepsake Cookies by Teri Pringle Wood, @teri_pringle_wood on Instagram.

Pages 131 and 133: Sasha Nicholas: Weave 24K Gold Dinner Plate with Couture Wreath Monogram in Navy, Weave 24K Gold Charger Plate with Couture Wreath Monogram in Navy; 888-877-5230, sashanicholas.com.

Pages 140–142: Royal Copenhagen: Star Fluted Christmas 22 cm Plate, Star Fluted Christmas 19 cm Plate, Star Fluted Christmas 39 cm Dish, Star Fluted Christmas Sugar Bowl, Star Fluted Christmas Teapot, Star Fluted Christmas 39 cl Jug, Star Fluted Christmas Cup and Saucer; royalcopenhagen.com.

Page 159: Special thanks to homeowner Mallory Smith, @mallorysmithinteriors on Instagram.

Page 162: Midori: Double Faced Satin Ribbon in Quince; 800-659-3049, midoriribbon.com.

Page 164: For more information about Donna Tronolone and Haverstraw Hill, visit her Instagram @haverstrawhill.

Pages 170–179: Place Royale, 2–4 Rue des Pains Bénits, Québec City, Québec, QC G1K, Canada, quebec-cite.com/en/

what-to-do-quebec-city/place-royale. Petit-Champlain, Québec City, Québec, Canada, quebecregion.com/en/old-quebec-summer/petit-champlain/. Basilique-Cathédrale Notre-Dame de Québec, 16 Rue de Buade, Québec, G1R 4A1, Canada, +1 418-692-2533, notre-dame-de-quebec.org. Plains of Abraham, 835 Wilfrid-Laurier Avenue, level 0, Québec City, G1R 2L3, Canada, +1 418-649-6157, ccbn-nbc.gc.ca. Fairmont Le Château Frontenac, 1 Rue des Carrières, Québec City, G1R 4P5, Canada,+1 418-692-3861, fairmont.com/frontenac-quebec/.

Pages 180–181 and 186: Church of Our Lady before Týn, Old Town Square, 110 00 Staré Město, Czechia, +420 222 318 186, tyn.cz.

Page 182: Rosenburg Palace, Jiřská, 119 00 Praha 1-Hradčany, Czechia.

Pages 183 and 186: St. Vitus Cathedral, III. nádvoří 48/2, Pražský hrad, 119 01 Praha 1-Hradčany, Czechia, +420 224 372 434, katedralasvatehovita.cz/cs.

Page 185: St. Nicholas Church in Lesser Town, Malostranské náměstí, Praha 1 – Malá Strana 118 00, Czechia, +420 257 534 215, stnicholas.cz.

Pages 188–195: The Hofburg, Michaelerkuppel, 1010 Vienna, Austria, +43 1 533 75 70, hofburg-wien.at. Hotel Sacher, Philharmoniker Str. 4. 1010 Vienna, Austria, +43 1 514560, sacher.com. Schönbrunn Palace, 1130 Vienna, Austria, +43 1 811 13 0, schoenbrunn.at. St. Michael's Church, Habsburgergasse 12, 1010 Vienna, Austria, +43 1 533 80 00, erzdioezese-wien.at/wien-St-Michael. St. Peter's Church, Petersplatz, 1010 Vienna, Austria, +43 1 533 64 33, peterskirche.at. St. Stephen's Cathedral, Stephansplatz 3, 1010 Vienna, Austria, +43 1 51552 3054, stephanskirche.at. Vienna Opera House, A Opernring 2, 1010 Vienna, Austria, +43 1 514 44 2250, wiener-staatsoper.at.

Pages 196–203: Paleis Het Loo, Koninklijk Park 1, 7315 JA Apeldoorn, Netherlands, +31 55 577 2400, paleishetloo.nl. Spirit of Winter, spiritofwinter.nl. Bilderberg Hotel De Keizerskroon, Koningstraat 7, 7315 HR Apeldoorn, Netherlands, +31 55 521 7744, bilderberg.nl/en/apeldoorn/hotel-de-keizerskroon. Aida's Atteljeeke, Passage 6A, 6301 DW Valkenburg aan de Geul, Netherlands, +31 6 40749414, aidasatteljeeke.nl. Bakkerij Geurten, Passage 13, 6301 DW, Valkenburg aan de Geul, Netherlands, +31 43 601 4584, bakkerijgeurten.nl. La Bonne Vie, Lindenlaan 10, 6301 HB Valkenburg, Netherlands.

Pages 206–213: Christ Church Cathedral, 2919 St. Charles Avenue, New Orleans, LA, 504-895-6602, cccnola.org. Immaculate Conception Jesuit Church, 130 Baronne Street, New Orleans, LA, 504-529-1477, jesuitchurch.net. St. Louis Cathedral, 615 Pere Antoine Alley, New Orleans, LA, 504-525-9585, stlouiscathedral.org. St. Patrick's Church, 724 Camp Street, New Orleans, LA, 504-525-4413, oldstpatricks.org.

Pages 220–221: Anabel Higgins Jewelry, anabelhiggins.com. Stamps & Stamps, 318 Fairview Avenue, South Pasadena, CA, 626-441-5600, stampsandstamps.com.

RECIPE INDEX